Poker Essays

By
Mason Malmuth

A product of Two Plus Two Publishing

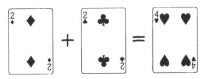

SECOND EDITION

SECOND PRINTING
DECEMBER 2000

Printing and Binding
Creel Printing Co.
Las Vegas, Nevada

Printed in the United States of America

POKER ESSAYS

Copyright © 1991, 1996, 2000 by Mason Malmuth.

For information contact:

Two Plus Two Publishing
226 Garfield Dr.
Henderson NV 89014
(702) 896-1326

ISBN: 1-880685-09-4

Table of Contents

About Mason Malmuth

Mason Malmuth was born and raised in Coral Gables, Florida. In 1973 he received his BS in Mathematics from Virginia Tech, and completed their Masters' program in 1975. While working for the United States Census Bureau in 1978, Mason stopped overnight in Las Vegas while driving to his new assignment in California. He was immediately fascinated by the games, and gambling became his major interest.

After arriving in California he discovered that poker was legal and began playing in some of the public cardrooms as well as taking periodic trips to Las Vegas where he would play both poker and blackjack. In 1981 he went to work for the Northrop Corporation as a mathematician and moved to Los Angeles where he could conveniently pursue his interest in poker in the large public cardrooms in Gardena, Bell Gardens, and Commerce.

In 1983 his first article "Card Domination — The Ultimate Blackjack Weapon" was published in *Gambling Times* magazine. In 1987 he left his job with the Northrop Corporation to begin a career as both a full-time gambler and a gambling writer. He has had over 500 articles published in various magazines and is the author or co-author of 13 books. These include *Gambling Theory and Other Topics,* where he tries to demonstrate why only a small number of people are highly successful at gambling. In this book he introduces the reader to the concept of "non-self weighting strategies" and explains why successful gambling is actually a balance of luck and skill. Other books he has co-authored are *Hold 'em Poker For Advanced Players,* written with David Sklansky, and *Seven-Card Stud For Advanced Players* written with David Sklansky and Ray Zee. All the "advanced" books are considered the definitive works on these games.

His company Two Plus Two Publishing has sold over 300,000 books and currently has 24 titles to its credit. These books are recognized as the best in their field and are thoroughly studied by those individuals who take gambling seriously.

Other Books by Mason Malmth

Gambling Theory and Other Topics
Blackjack Essays
Poker Essays, Volume II
Winning Concepts in Draw and Lowball

Gambling for a Living by David Sklansky and Mason Malmuth
Hold 'em Poker for Advanced Players by David Sklansky and Mason Malmuth
Seven-Card Stud for Advanced Players by David Sklansky, Mason Malmuth, and Ray Zee
The Professional Poker Dealer's Handbook by Dan Paymar, Donna Harris, and Mason Malmuth

Booklets with Mason Malmuth

Fundamentals of Craps by Mason Malmuth and Lynne Loomis
Fundamentals of Poker by Mason Malmuth and Lynne Loomis
Fundamentals of "21" by Mason Malmuth and Lynne Loomis
Fundamentals of Video Poker by Mason Malmuth and Lynne Loomis

Introduction

What's the most important thing that a serious poker player should do? Use good discipline? Become knowledgeable about the game? Select the best game? Read all the good poker books? Know his opponents? Play tight? Or, something else?

I believe it is something else, and that something else is to think about the game and to constantly try to adjust and improve his level of play. There is no doubt in my mind that the biggest downfall of most people who attempt to play poker seriously is their failure to analyze what happens to them when they are sitting at the poker tables.

Thinking, then, is the theme of this book, and we will explore many ideas that should be new to most readers. Some of these ideas come from my other books, especially *Gambling Theory and Other Topics*. Other ideas come from projects I am currently involved in, and a few of the concepts discussed are based on feedback and comments from other people. Some of this material may prove challenging for many readers, but I have tried to write in such a way that most everyone should be able to understand what I am talking about.

In addition, I want to point out that much of this material has been published previously. Many of the essays in this book are rewrites of my columns that appeared in *The Card Player*. But even if you already have read some of the material, this book still should be beneficial.

Some of what follows also is quite controversial. I sometimes jokingly tell my friends that the reason I write is to try to irritate as many people as possible. A few of the essays in this book did seem to have that effect. However, my main reason for addressing certain subjects is to promote thinking and discussion. In this sense, I believe I was successful. But keep in mind that some of what follows are just my opinions, and my opinions are not always absolutely correct.

1

Another thing to consider is that in a sense, poker is a game of levels. In other words, the skills that are very important at one level of play become trivial at another.

For example, when you first start out, certain mechanical skills, such as holding your cards so that no one else can see them, are extremely important. However, after you have played for a while, this idea becomes trivial, since keeping your cards concealed should be automatic.

I believe this is especially true when you reach the very advanced level of play where you are trying to put your head into someone's else's head and see what he is thinking. This is what really separates the great players from those who just play well. It also allows the great players to be "sloppy" in certain other areas. This is probably why certain individuals, who seem to play bad, really do quite well.

One thing I have tried to do in this book is to present poker. A problem with the gambling literature in general, and with some of the poker literature in particular, is that a significant emphasis is placed on the terrific qualities of the individual author. Specifically, I don't claim to have a whole allegiance of students who "faithfully follow their master," and I don't claim to have won all the money in the world. I do, however, try to present facts and ideas that I think are well worth reading and examining.

Finally, I would like to thank a few friends for helping me put much of this material together. They include David Sklansky, Ray Zee, Ed Hill, Mark Weitzman, Dan Harrington, and many others. I also want to thank June Field and the entire *Card Player* staff for putting up with me and being willing to publish many of my ideas. In addition, I'd like to express my appreciation to Lynne Loomis for her work in editing this manuscript. Thanks to her, most of you will not only be able to read this book, but to understand it as well.

Part One

General Concepts

General Concepts

Introduction

When I first began to play poker, I believed it would be easy. Being a professional mathematician, I thought I would quickly memorize a preset strategy, as the blackjack experts do, and then simply never lose. Was I in for a surprise! This game was just too complicated.

Learning to become an expert poker player can take a lifetime. This is especially true if your game is hold'em or stud. But even relatively easy games like razz or high draw aren't really as simple as they first appear.

In many aspects, poker is a way of life. You don't become an expert poker player overnight, and you don't become an expert poker player by just occasionally thinking about the game. In fact, as we shall see, poker includes many things that someone new to the game might not consider relevant.

The ideas discussed in this section won't make you a winner. On the other hand, without a complete understanding of these topics, you won't have any chance to be a winner. Let's get started.

The Worst Plays in History

I've been playing poker for a number of years now and I have seen a lot of terrible plays. But two of them for some reason seem to stand out in my mind. Since both plays are also somewhat humorous, I thought I would share them with you.

Play No. 1: Who's on first. This play occurred in one of the major poker rooms in Las Vegas. The game was $10-$20 hold'em, and there was a fairly large multiway pot at the beginning of the hand. But at the end, only two players were left. The board showed:

After the river card was placed on the board, the player who was second to act bet. "Wait a minute," yelled the other player. "I'm first."

The dealer then told the out-of-turn player that he would have to take his bet back and let his opponent act. This was done, and then the first player bet. After a short pause, the out-of-turn bettor threw his hand away. "I knew I had you," announced the "new" bettor, as he showed everyone at the table the:

5

Play No. 2: The triple-pot syndrome. Before the advent of stud and hold'em in Southern California, and before I moved to Las Vegas, one of the games I often played was $50-$100 draw, jacks or better to open, which was spread three or four nights a week at the Bicycle Club. (Sadly, the big high-draw games are all just about gone. They became victims of a form of poker, known as Texas hold'em, that has much more action. Also, in high draw, unlike in lowball, a weak player usually would lose all his money quickly. These games were very profitable when the competition was not too tough.) To understand the following terrible play, you need to understand the way this game was structured. It was generally eight-handed, and everyone would ante $10. Depending on the game, the pot would not be opened from one-fourth to one-third of the time. When this happened, everyone would ante another $10, but the limits remained at $50-$100. If again no one opened, there would be one last $10 ante, and the limits would now double to $100-$200.

Even though we saw a lot of double pots, there were very few triple pots. This was because the total ante in the double pots was so large compared to the size of the bet that most players would open on anything — including a pair of jacks — that was eligible no matter what their position. In addition, they would seldom sandbag any hand.

One night after I sat down, a live one who showed up about once a week announced to the table that he liked to play triple pots. I assumed that he must have won a triple pot just before I sat down, since he had a lot of chips in front of him. Anyway, after playing for a few minutes, a double pot came up where this particular player had the button. Everyone passed to him, meaning that there was a very good chance that no hands were out, and to my amazement, our hero turned over his hand. He held:

"I like to play triple pots," he announced, as he threw his hand to the dealer.

Final Note. There is something to be learned from these two stories. It is the fact that some of your opponents have little conception of what they are doing. Always be on the lookout for these players, and try to make an effort to get into their games. (In addition, try to sit as close to them as possible, preferably on their left, so you will be in lots of hands with them.) Terrible players don't come along that often, but when they show up, they make things very worthwhile. By the way, some of these people have years of playing experience, but for some reason, they still are completely unaware when they sit down at the poker table.

Jackpot Games:
Another Look

Are jackpot games worth playing? Does the additional rake make these games just too expensive to be profitable? Can a professional player on a small bankroll survive playing in jackpot games if he doesn't hit a jackpot? Are these games ruining poker?

For readers who don't know, jackpot games are those where an additional "drop" is taken from each pot, and the accumulated money, or "jackpot," is then eventually returned to the lucky player who has a very powerful hand beaten, such as six-four in lowball or aces full in hold'em. Recently, there have been jackpots as large as $50,000 at some of the California cardrooms. Needless to say, when jackpots get this high, they are a great "drawing card" for the particular cardrooms that have them.

But the question often arises as to whether a regular player, assuming that he does not hit a jackpot, can beat these games on a day-in, day-out basis. In *Winning Concepts in Draw and Lowball*, I have a section devoted to jackpot games. In this section I argue that these games are good for the serious (low-limit) player, because the possibility of winning a jackpot would make many typical opponents play very badly. What happens is that many players begin to play too many hands, such as two-card draws in lowball and any pair in hold'em, in situations where these hands are clearly unprofitable to play (not considering the jackpot). Consequently, the solid player will benefit from this loose action. In addition, some players go into a survival mode to ensure that they will have enough chips to play a few extra hands and possibly win a jackpot. Specifically, they do not bet for value in situations where it is obvious to do so, simply because the extra bet they might lose may cost them a chance at a jackpot if this loss means that they might go broke sooner. Needless to say, this type of play is also highly advantageous to the skilled player.

8

But there has been a major change in most cardrooms since I wrote *Winning Concepts in Draw and Lowball.* Jackpots are now much larger. There is, of course, no problem with having bigger jackpots. But to have bigger jackpots, the clubs need to drop much more than they used to, and to those of you trying to survive, this additional money taken from the pots can be very important. In fact, someone just surviving before may now be looking at a shrinking bankroll.

One meaningful question is whether this additional drop, meaning bigger jackpots, makes typical players play even worse than the original jackpots did. I can answer this question only with an opinion, and this opinion is no. It seems as though the small jackpots were enough to make many typical opponents play very poorly, and it is hard for me to imagine that a significantly larger jackpot can make some of these people play any worse. If this is the case, those of you on a small bankroll who are playing seriously in the small-limit games, are being hurt by the large jackpots currently available.

But there is another side to this story. Even though I believe what I have written is correct, jackpot games are still good for those who play very well. I have an acquaintance, who I think is a good player but not a great player, who has spent the last year and a half playing $5-$10 hold'em games, which are also jackpot games, in Southern California. During this time, he has averaged approximately $12 per hour and plays a full 40 hours a week. Now $12 per hour won't make you rich in our modern times, but it definitely says these games can be beaten, even with their significant drops, and even if you don't hit a jackpot.

Finally, I don't believe jackpot games are ruining poker. In fact, they may be having just the opposite effect if they encourage more people to play, and I suspect that this is the case. However, because of the large jackpot drop, fewer people probably "graduate" to the middle-limit games, and this may not be good for poker in the long run.

The Cost of Poker

What does it really cost to sit at a poker table? Is it as expensive as some people say? Or is playing poker a bargain? When I say cost, I'm not talking about the rake or tips. These things I consider as extra costs. What I'm referring to is how much money you put into the pot in blinds, antes, and forced bring-ins just to have the option of playing your hand. I'm writing about this topic not because I regard it as very important — I don't — but because I have read several articles recently that were just plain wrong, and I thought I should correct those misconceptions.

Specifically, suppose you are playing $10-$20 hold'em. Let's assume that you get to play four full rounds (40 hands) per hour. Since you are forced to post a $10 blind and a $5 blind each round, for a total of $15, it appears that just to sit at the poker table costs you $60 an hour, and to be a winning player, you must win back that $60 plus a little extra. Seems like the game is pretty expensive.

Even though I have seen something similar to this written many times, it is just not correct. The reason it is wrong is that you sometimes get free plays in the big blind. For example, suppose you hold a hand in the big blind that you think is worth $4. If you had to post a full bet, you would never play. However, since your money is already posted, and since your hand is worth $4, it is actually only costing you $6 to play, not $10 as most people think.

Consequently, $10-$20 hold'em does not cost $60 an hour to play. And since this idea carries over to other forms of poker where there is a blind or a forced bring-in, games like Omaha, lowball, and seven-card stud are also not as "expensive" as some people believe.

This reminds me of a related idea. I once met a player at the hold'em table who carried a little notebook with him and recorded the results of every hand he played. "Mason," he said, "it's amazing, but I show a profit when I play a pair of deuces." "Well," I replied, "if you are trying to play correctly, why would you play a hand that didn't show a profit?"

I think my point is obvious. *If you play poker to win, you should virtually never play a hand unless it has positive expectation.* Even playing a few hands that you know are unprofitable can turn you from a winner into a loser, especially if some of these bad hands are more unprofitable than you think.

By the way, the reason I said "virtually" never play a hand unless it has positive expectation is that it is sometimes correct to play a bad hand or to play a hand badly just to throw your opponents off, so you can trap them or get them to make some sort of costly mistake against you later in the game. This is especially true in no-limit, where if a small error on your part gets your opponent to make a large error later on, your expectation can be enormous.

However, in limit play, while this sort of strategy does have some value, I recommend that it be restricted to only those hands where the cost is small but the mistake looks obvious to your opponents. An example from seven-card stud might be to reraise an obvious pair of queens when you have a pair of sevens with an ace kicker if your hand is extremely live, and if you were going to play anyway, and if you also planned on going to the river as long as your hand remained live and your opponent's board did not look too scary.

Handling Pressure

If you gamble, especially if you play poker, to be successful you must be able to handle the pressure associated with the swings and other undesirable game conditions (like an occasional obnoxious opponent). Those of you who are unable to do this will be only marginally successful at best, and at worst will go broke very quickly.

One apparent way to avoid too much pressure is to not play in games that are too big for you. In this context, I'm not referring to the size of the game in relation to your bankroll, but to that psychological number each of us has. However, it should be obvious to most readers that playing with your rent money is not a way to reduce pressure. Needless to say, those of you who put themselves in this type of situation just invite disaster, and I see people doing this sort of thing all the time.

One question that arises is how to determine whether you are effectively handling the pressure associated with the game you are in? An easy way to tell is by observing your own behavior and comparing it to the behavior of those people you know who consistently do well. If you find yourself constantly throwing cards or lecturing your opponent about how stupid his play was, then you should probably go to a smaller game. Other possible signs of an inability to handle pressure are constantly thinking that you are being cheated, believing that the dealers are shorting the pot or palming chips, or being unable to get along with most of the floor people or the players that you are up against.

Of course, I may be describing someone who has more serious problems than too much pressure, and I am certainly not an expert in this area. On the other hand, I see very few winning players who exhibit these behavior patterns, and I do believe that being able to handle the situations they are in contributes to their success.

Obviously, the result of not being able to handle pressure will be major mistakes in your play. We poker players call this "going on tilt" or "steaming," and we love to play against opponents who are out of control. Sometimes these steaming opponents can't give their money away fast enough. (Being afraid of the stakes also may cause you to play too passively, which can be just as expensive in the long run.)

In my opinion, one of the best ways to handle pressure is to make sure that you play well. It is much easier to handle the swings associated with poker if you are absolutely certain you are a very good player than if you just hope that you are.

So how do you become a very good player? First, study the small number of good books that are available. (See the appendixes at the back of this book for recommended reading, or see *Gambling Theory and Other Topics* for extensive reviews of many poker texts.) Second, try to get an expert player to talk to you about how to play. This has helped me tremendously. Just be sure that you are talking to an expert instead of someone who just thinks he plays well. Third, get lots of playing experience. You don't become a great poker player overnight; it does take some time. And fourth, spend as much time as possible thinking about the game, including hands you have already played, how your opponents perceive you, and how to adjust your strategy against different types of opponents.

Changing the subject slightly, I believe that some pressure is needed to ensure good play. How many of you find yourselves successful in a limit like $20-$40 but are unable to win in a limit like $3-$6? I find this true of myself. The size of the stakes has to have some meaning, or it is difficult to play your best; the game just becomes too boring.

Being Unaware

The other day while waiting to get into a hold'em game, I observed the following play. There was a multiway pot, and the flop came:

Two players got into a raising war, with a third player caught in the middle. A blank hit on the turn, and the raising war resumed, with the third player just calling. Obviously there were two threes out, but almost just as obvious was that the player caught in the middle held two sevens which gave him a full house. Although I have seen this kind of play many times, it still amazes me how completely unaware many poker players are, even those who play for serious money.

But even more amazing when I talk to those players who I consider unaware, they will tell me just the opposite: "I watch every move every player makes." "Nothing gets by me!" "I know what every card means." Yet in many cases, it seems as though everything gets by certain players, especially on their most important hands.

So what causes this? I think it is simply that in important situations, many poker players get so caught up in the action that they totally forget what is going on. In stud, I have seen people put in far too many raises with an ace-high flush when an ace-king flush was plainly visible in an opponent's hand. In razz, I have seen players with a possible second-best hand raise out opponents who were clearly drawing dead. And in draw lowball, I have seen people with a rough pat seven raise so many times that an opponent broke

14

an eight, and they were aware that this opponent even had an eight in his hand.

A way to avoid this problem is to spend a great deal of time thinking about the game. Then when a major confrontation develops, you may have played it through your mind at least once before — or perhaps you have thought through something similar — and you already might know what to do. I think this is one of the real keys to playing successful winning poker, but I know of very few players who regularly utilize it. Those who do, however, are big winners.

What usually happens is that the typical player looks at his hand and gets excited if it is a quality holding. Then he plays his hand very strongly, never thinking that this strong play may be costing him money. If only it were possible to step back from the game and think things through, this person might realize that a different strategy is better.

What I suggest for an aspiring poker player is to try to remember those hands, whether you won or lost them, that developed into major confrontations. After your playing session, think the whole hand through, remembering exactly how you played it and also examining any alternate strategies that might be available. Also think about how your opponent played his hand. What you might discover is that even though you may have won a big pot, there was a better way to play the hand, or you may realize that an alternate strategy might have saved you a bet or perhaps even the pot. In addition, you may discover that your opponent made an error that allowed you to win more or to lose less than you were supposed to.

An obvious illustration is the lowball example given earlier. If you hold a pat seven, and you know your opponent holds a pat eight, don't put in too many raises. By thinking things through, you may realize that winning a medium-sized pot all the time is better than winning a large pot most of the time but also occasionally losing that large pot.

Evaluating Yourself and Your Opponents

In the poker world, very few players will admit that someone else plays better than they do. I have even been told about all the "suckers" that have won some of the major tournaments. Somehow I tend to think that all of these people can play. At least they seem to do a pretty good job in the tournaments, and I am not real eager to have most of them in my games.

I believe one reason why players can't admit their own shortcomings is that poker seems to attract a lot of people with big egos. If you have trouble admitting (1) that you don't play as well as you think you do, or (2) that some of your opponents play very well, perhaps even better than you do, then you are simply costing yourself money. Accurate evaluation of your play and of the games you are in is one of the key ingredients to success in the poker world.

But I believe there is another reason why so many people think that no one else can play well. It has to do with the fact that very sophisticated plays can look bad to someone who does not understand them. This is especially true when these plays don't work, or if these plays are something that you would never attempt. In fact, it is easy to sometimes think that a world-class player is a complete idiot.

Here's an example from seven-card stud. Suppose you, a world-class player try to steal the pot with a very marginal hand, perhaps a small pair. Everyone passes except the last player, who raises. However, you think this player may have realized that you might be on a steal and may be trying to resteal himself. Thus you reraise, only to get raised again. Now you know that either you are up against a very big hand or your small pair is good. Consequently, you call. If it turns out that you are up against a big hand, your call certainly won't look like much of a play, especially to someone who doesn't understand what has happened.

16

Here's another example from hold'em. A tight player raises and is called by three other tight players. You are in the big blind with:

Pretty terrible hand, isn't it? The type that you should immediately throw away. Well, not necessarily.

Notice that since all of your opponents are tight, there is a good chance that a bunch of high cards are used up. Also notice that if you get lucky and hit your hand, it easily could be the best hand on the flop, and you could win a pretty big pot.

Of course, this play requires a lot of sophistication. Not only do you need to know your opponents extremely well, but also you must be willing to look quite foolish when your hand is no good, and you must be willing to invest some chips.

Here's a final example from seven-card stud. You are in a two-handed pot, and your opponent has an exposed pair of kings. However, you put him on a draw, and this is all you think he has. Unfortunately, your draw also missed, and you cannot beat his exposed pair. This might be a good time to try for a bluff, since you can reason that your opponent will think you obviously can beat his board and probably can beat two pair. On the other hand, if you are called and are beaten by just his pair of kings, some of the players at your table probably will think you can't play. "He couldn't even beat a pair of kings," they will think. "What a dumb bet."

Getting back to the original theme of this essay, when I sit down in a game, I immediately try to figure out who plays well. Knowing this alone makes a difference in my play. Obviously, I try to play a little tighter against the experts and try to get into fewer pots with them, especially if I hold a marginal hand. Simply put, they are usually the ones that I concentrate on.

Computer Games — Why They Are So Bad

I've recently spent a little time looking at several computer poker games. All of these games allow you to play at a full table, where you control the decisions of your hand, and the computer controls the decisions of the other hands. I suspect that we will be seeing a lot of these games in the future, and at this moment, I have some definite opinions on them — opinions that I think will surprise most readers.

Are these computer poker games any good? Should we all run out and buy them? Will playing them sharpen our skills? My answer is to all three questions is no. *In fact, all of the games I have looked at are absolutely terrible!*

Why are these games so bad? Why is it that what happens at the poker table cannot be duplicated, even though the creators of these games obviously have spent a lot of time working on their products? Let's take a look.

When I talk to some of the top players about how to play certain hands, I am always asked two questions: "How well do you play compared to your opponent?" and "How much control do you have over this opponent?" What this means is that to play poker well, you must adjust your strategy depending on who you are against, what you think of their play, and what you think they think of your play. This is especially true in games like hold'em and stud. It is also true, but to a lesser extent, in games like high draw and lowball. In other words, to play really well, you can't just be on "automatic pilot."

All of the computer games I have looked at have several weaknesses. First, each opponent appears to have just one strategy. The computer opponent opens with certain hands (in certain positions), calls with certain hands, bets certain hands, throws away certain hands, and so forth. The computer strategy seems to be completely fixed, and there is just no flexibility. That is, the computer is unable to learn who is tight and who is loose, who is aggressive and who is passive, who might be steaming and who is currently playing at his best, or any other variants.

For example, in *Hold'em Poker For Advanced Players* David Sklansky and I state that in early position, you should play hands in Groups I-IV if the game is typical, hands in Groups I-V if the game is weak, and only hands in Groups I-III if the game is tough. None of the computer games I have looked at have even this simple capability.

The second area of weakness is that too much emphasis is put on first-round play. (This is before the flop in hold'em and on third street in seven-card stud.) There is no question that first-round play is important, but mistakes made in a late round can be terrible, especially if they cost you the pot or several large bets. For example, in one computer hold'em game I watched, a pair of fives got into a raising war on the river with another (computer) opponent. Finally the pair of fives called. It could not beat the board.

This leads to another weakness. The computer opponents do not seem capable of learning from the action that has already taken place. For instance, in the example just given any halfway knowledgeable player should have been able to deduce that he was probably beat sometime in the hand. Even tourists who have very little poker experience won't lose as much on this type of hand as the computer managed to lose.

A related point is that the computer seems unable to glean anything from the cards that are out or from the previous action. Knowledge of this type can dramatically change how a hand should be played. In fact, it can transform a very strong hand into a weak one, or vice versa, and it may allow you to gain or save bets as the hand progresses. The programs I have looked at seem completely lacking in this area.

Finally, I also question the ability and knowledge of the creators of these computer games. I am not talking about their ability to write programs. In fact, the graphics and many of the options and features the programs have are quite impressive. What I'm referring to is their lack of understanding of the poker games themselves. For instance, in the documentation for one computer hold'em game, the author described what it was that made a hand good. The emphasis was completely on high cards, which is, of course, important. However, he did not appear to understand the distinction between suited and unsuited hands, or to understand the impact that many opponents — as opposed to the pot being contested short-handed — have on the strength of particular holdings.

Perhaps there will be better poker computer games sometime in the future. But I tend to doubt it. I suspect that poker is just too difficult a game to program reasonably well.

Poker Magic

I recently started rereading *Sklansky on Poker Theory*, a book I have read many times before. Today, an expanded version of this book is available under the new title of *The Theory of Poker*. In addition, David Sklansky has rewritten much of the material in the book so that it is easier to understand.

I would like, however to quote a little bit of the introduction from the original version:

> I am a firm believer in the fact that *before you can even think of using tricks and ploys you must be an excellent player.* Those players who are good hustlers but aren't good players will not get the money if they are up against tough competition. This book is specifically for those players who are playing in tough games. However, it should be obvious that any player who can beat tough games will have little trouble in destroying easier games. In tough games, something like putting a submarine sandwich in the pot when you know your opponents are hungry, as one poker authority recommends, just isn't going to do it.

The reason I quoted this paragraph is that Sklansky states something that is extremely important: *You do not become a winning poker player by some quick magic formula or by becoming highly skilled in just one or two aspects of the game.* Poker is a very complex game, and winning at poker is hard work. There are not a small number of tricks that you can pick up and be "guaranteed an income for life." You simply must play better than most of your opponents in just about all areas that come under the heading of poker. Keep in mind that some of your opponents also may play very well.

At the time of this writing, David Sklansky, Ray Zee, and I have just finished the text for our book, *Seven-Card Stud For Advanced*

Players. To write the text, we first developed a set of notes that was more than 60 typed pages long. In a sense, someone who has studied our stud material will sit down at the table with the equivalent of 60 mental pages on how to play stud.

This brings up an interesting question. How many (mental) pages does the average person have? I'm not sure, but I suspect that it is typically less than half that amount. Now when someone who plays with only 20 to 30 (mental) pages compares himself to someone who plays with more than twice as many it will appear that he is up against a magician. "How does he do it?" the average player will wonder. "I sure wish I held as many cards as he does."

Here's another way of expressing this. You do not get to be a great player because you are aggressive, know the percentages, have the proper image, recognize a lot of tells, are good at reading hands, can manipulate your opponents into mistakes, don't play too loose or too tight, have a good understanding of people, know your particular opponents well, have years of experience, check raise at the proper times, are good at buying free cards, select good games, can also play well short handed, etc. You become a great player because you excel in all of these things and a lot more, and because you are able to combine them in the proper mix.

When reading the poker literature, I sometimes get the impression that a few writers put too much emphasis on one certain skill. Perhaps they recently raised and bought themselves a free card which allowed them to win a big pot. That doesn't mean that this is all there is to it. As stated earlier, the best and most successful poker players are very well-rounded and highly skilled. They know how to adjust their games to the situation. (In fact, they are constantly adjusting their play so that they can stay one step ahead of their opponents.) There is not a magic formula (or a few things that they emphasize) that allows them to win wheelbarrows full of money. It is mostly hard work and the slow process of accumulating a great deal of knowledge that permits them to be so successful.

This means that if you are starting out in poker, don't expect to be a world-class player overnight. But with time and hard work, it can be accomplished.

What's Not Important

Recently, I received a letter from someone inquiring about poker lessons. I found the letter more interesting than most I receive because of the things the writer requested help with:

- Developing more patience, discipline, and attentiveness
- Learning to pause and make each decision before acting (act, not react).
- Acting naturally, so as not to give away tells
- Looking for tells and using them.
- Using past behavior and frequency counts to interpret current behavior and anticipate future behavior
- Establishing, maintaining, and regaining emotional control

What I find interesting about this is that virtually none of it is very important. Obviously, I am dealing with someone who is new to poker and who has fallen into what I call the "magic formula trap." Simply put, if you don't have a good understanding of how to play poker correctly, it won't help if you are an expert in all of these things. In other words, you can expect to go broke.

Let me be specific. If you are a stud player, and you consistently play hands that are not live, or you play small pairs regardless of your kicker, expect to go broke. Similarly, in hold'em, if you insist on calling raises with hands like

don't expect to do very well.

To be a successful poker player, you must have a good "basic strategy" on which your game is built. However, don't let the term "basic strategy" deceive you. Poker is a very complex game. (This is especially true if your form of poker is Texas hold'em or seven-card stud.) This means that what I call basic strategy is also very complex. In fact, if you are relatively new to poker, developing a sound basic strategy is where you should concentrate your efforts.

I believe that if you develop a good understanding of the game, most of these things listed above will take care of themselves. However, emphasizing those areas, especially too early in your poker career, can keep you from gaining a complete understanding of the game, and you probably will never achieve the level of success that the true experts do.

Specifically, if you understand how to play well and learn to execute the right plays at the right time, patience, discipline, and alertness will take care of themselves. You won't need to pause and take a lot of time to consider each decision, because will you already have a good idea of what to do. Since your decisions will be strategically strong, you will gain confidence, and this will help you to eliminate tells.

As for tells, I believe that even though they are valuable, their significance has been overemphasized. In any case, it doesn't take long to learn the basic concepts behind winning tell play. Also, in the more complex games like Texas hold'em and seven-card stud, tells seem to be less important than they are in the simpler games, such as high draw and razz.

Frequency counts and past behavior can be of value, but they also can be deceptive. Understanding exactly how your opponents play is not only important, but also absolutely essential to winning play. On the other hand, the distribution of hands you receive in a short period of time can vary widely. Someone who appears loose based on the numbers of hands he plays in a short period of time in reality may be a very tight player. In addition, highly skilled players occasionally may deliberately misplay a hand just to throw you off at some future time. Again, the way you overcome this is to develop a good understanding of how the game should be played.

And finally, emotional control also is aided by a thorough understanding of how the game should be played. Part of the reason why some players steam their money away is because they make plays that are strategically wrong, or they are unable to recognize expert plays their opponents make against them. It is true that the large, short-term luck factor present in almost all forms of poker can discourage even the best players at times, but these players are also the individuals who seem to be in the most control of themselves.

The World's Worst Player

I've done some speculating with a few friends recently, trying to guess how much the world's worst player is supposed to lose. Specifically, suppose you are playing in a "typical" $10-$20 hold'em game, and seated at the table is a player who (1) plays every hand, (2) always goes to the river, and (3) never raises unless he has the absolute "nuts." (This means that if you are raised, you always can safely throw your hand away.) How much do you think this person is expected to lose per hour?

Even though it is only a guess, our conclusion was that this person has an expectation of minus $150 per hour. Now this doesn't mean that he won't occasionally walk away from the table a winner, but it does mean that in the long run, his overall results will be quite horrendous.

By the way, I don't see very many people playing this badly. Those who do either quickly go broke or their game quickly improves. However, you do occasionally see a "tourist" who plays almost this poorly.

Now suppose you have two of these world's worst players in a game, and everyone else plays about equally. This means that the other eight players should expect to split from $200 to $240 per hour, depending on the rake and/or time charge. In other words, if you are one of the lucky ones sitting in this game, your win rate should be between $25 and $30 per hour.

If you also are an expert player, your win rate (in this game) easily could be around $50 per hour. Not bad considering there are only two bad players out of the 10.

This brings up an interesting point, which is also an extremely important concept for those of you who are seriously trying to make money playing poker. When selecting a game, try to determine how terrible the worst players in the game really do play. It is highly doubtful that they will play as badly as the "world's worst player." But the point is, even if a game has several very good players in it, it still may be worth playing if it also has a couple of very bad players in it. Don't necessarily let a couple of experts scare you off. On the other hand, a game that has all mediocre players may not be worth very much, even if you are superior to everyone at the table. The reason for this is simple: You win most of your money (in the long run) from the very bad players, not from those who play only a little worse than you.

In my opinion, this is a major cause of the downfall of many professional players. They look at a game, think they are at least as good as, or perhaps better than, anyone seated, and join the action. Not only do their egos sometimes cause them to overrate themselves, but even if they are right, they still might be better off in another game. They just fail to understand where the real money comes from in poker. Assuming that you are extremely good, you can win a little from those who play OK, but you win a lot from those who play terrible.

This reminds me of an observation I made several years ago. I was watching a big no-limit game at one of the major tournaments. The blinds were $25-$25-$25, and there was just one live player in the game. But this player was so live that he made it worthwhile for everyone in the game. This included those who really didn't play that well when compared to the experts.

After a few minutes, a new game was called down with blinds of $25-$25-$50, and the extremely live player announced that he was going to it. A friend of mine, who is a world-class player, was also in the original game. He immediately grabbed his chips and ran to the new table. Even though he was clearly the best player in the original game, my friend told me later that without the live one he was "better off sleeping."

I learned a lot from that experience. It's often not how well you play, but how badly some of your opponents play. In fact, once you learn to play reasonably well, how well you play may not really be that important anymore. This sounds like a contradiction, and it is certainly true that if you play poorly, your lack of skill definitely will influence your results. But if you do play well, how badly some of your opponents play may be much more important in determining your overall expectation.

Lending Money

Constantly being asked for money by other players, who have absolutely no intention of paying it back is only one of the many problems that people in the poker world face. A friend of mine recently told me that he saw someone who owed him $20 cashing in several racks of $5 chips. Can I get my $20 back?" my friend asked. If you can't guess, the answer was, "No."

Several years ago, I lent $300 to a "very nice lady" with whom I had played poker perhaps 200 times in the previous 18 months (at one of the major clubs in Los Angeles). Needless to say, I never saw her again. Now she didn't quit playing poker; One of my friends saw her several times in another cardroom across town. But apparently, she was willing to drive an extra 20 miles a day rather than to pay me back.

By the way, as this story shows, a good way to get rid of pests (in the poker world) is to lend them money. Usually $5 or $10 will do the trick. You don't have to be as generous as I was.

There are other ways that unethical poker players extract money from fellow players. Perhaps the most common is to talk someone into either staking them or taking a piece of their action. Then they just report a loss (which did not occur). My advice is not to stake anyone or take a piece of someone unless you know him extremely well. Most people who are looking for a stake or for a partner are honest. But plenty of money is stolen from naive players in this way, so you should be very sure about the integrity of the person you are dealing with.

For example, I've been told of a player (now deceased) who regularly sold more than 100 percent of himself in tournaments. Of course, he usually never finished in the money. But the one time he did manage to win a tournament, instead of paying his partners, this player supposedly faked a heart attack and immediately had to be taken from the poker room in an ambulance.

29

When this person died a couple of years ago, I couldn't help but wonder if his death also was faked. If this was the case, he would not have to pay back all the people to whom he owed money.

Actually, I could tell you a lot of stories along these lines. But I won't. Those of you who are new to the poker world should be very cautious about financing "expert" players. I know of several people who have made a fair amount of money playing tournaments. Nothing wrong with that. The only problem is that the people who have put them in those tournaments are far behind. (This is because the person who is staked collects when he finishes in the money but doesn't lose anything when he is eliminated early. On the other hand, the person putting up the money collects only a percentage of the win when money is made but loses it all when no money gets returned.)

Again, I don't want to imply that every person who sits across the poker table from you is a cheat or a crook or what is known as a welsh. In fact, the majority of people I know who play poker seriously are quite honest. But there are still enough players who do unethical things, like borrow money with no intention of ever repaying it, that it is wise to be cautious.

Craving Action

To demonstrate a point, I'd like to tell a little poker story. (Not a bad-beat story!) I was playing in a $15-$30 razz game a while back in Las Vegas. I had sat in the game for more than 40 minutes, but with the exception of the forced bring-in, I had not played a hand. Now, even though this particular game has a small ante structure — meaning that tight play is correct — the real reason I had not voluntarily entered a pot yet was that I hadn't picked up anything playable. Simply put, I was not catching any cards.

Finally, I had a worthwhile hand, and after a king brought it in for $5, I made the bet $15. "Look, Mason finally played a hand," said the player with the king up. "It's taken him almost an hour to find something." Well, to my amazement, this player called, and we played a pot heads-up.

The reason I tell this story is not to point out how long you can sometimes sit between playable hands, but to illustrate that many opponents simply make terrible plays. It is this type of opponent (along with some other types that I will not discuss here) who make the games very profitable. Actually, the person who called me is really a fairly good player who just called my bet as a joke. But the point is that many bad players consistently make these types of plays, and they know very well that they are costing themselves money.

This brings up an interesting point. If they know these plays are bad, then why do they make them. The only reason I can think of is that many players crave action, and the thrill of being in action is enough to keep them playing.

One thing that is very important in these situations is to make sure that your terrible-playing opponents keep making these costly plays. The best way to do this is to try to appear as though you are gambling with them. Also, don't comment on their play, and don't ridicule or needle them. In other words, keep your mouth shut.

One form of needling, which is very popular among struggling professional players, is to ask to see their opponent's cards when the hand is over. Perhaps our struggling pro will learn how his opponent plays. But in reality, all he will do is embarrass the live one into playing much better. I have seen many good games ruined when some "expert" forces all the live ones to play better, simply because he shows the world how terrible they play and makes sure that they quit gambling. Even worse is the expert who explains in detail, usually when he is mad, why his opponent's play was so terrible. This can cause the live ones to be driven out of the games altogether, and I can't think of anything worse that can happen.

By the way, as I have mentioned in some of my other writings, the large, short-term luck factor present in poker hooks the live ones into making some of these terrible plays. So be happy when they do draw out on you. Remember, if they never did administer a bad beat, they never would play so stupidly in the first place.

A corollary to these ideas is to try to never do anything in a poker game that might get the live ones out of a gambling mood. This topic could fill several pages, and I won't go into it here. However, keep in mind that anything you do that may make your "live" opponents play tighter could be very costly. In fact, it can turn profitable games into unprofitable games for many so-called "professional" players.

Staying Broke

I have a couple of friends who play poker fairly well, yet they always seem to keep themselves broke. Although they have trouble understanding why they never have any money, in my opinion, they seem to consistently fall into several traps that keep them on or near the rail. They are not the only ones who fall into these traps; many otherwise skilled players also manage to keep themselves broke. What is interesting is that these traps are difficult to break out of even if you play at an expert level.

Trap No. 1: Always looking for the big score. Suppose you have a bankroll of only $1,000. A $1,000 win would be pretty good; it would double your bankroll. But a $1,000 loss, which would cause you to become broke, would be disastrous. Yet I see people taking these double-or-nothing risks all the time. They do it either by entering tournaments or by taking shots in games that are way too big for them. It's true that occasionally someone who is virtually broke takes a shot and comes out a winner. But in my opinion, when you are on a small bankroll, you should be content to "grind." The time to gamble is when you can afford to lose the money.

In fact, as I show in *Gambling Theory And Other Topics*, those who insist on constant adventuring will stay broke. This is because the standard deviation (the statistical measure of short-term luck) in poker is so large that a relatively large loss is inevitable sooner or later. If this relatively large loss occurs in a game that is "too big," expect to be broke or at least close to it.

Trap No. 2: Underestimating the competition in the big games. Let's suppose you are a fairly decent player. Perhaps you are a modest winner in the $10-$20 hold'em games. Now you observe a game that looks great because there appear to be a couple of awful players in it. The problem is that the game is a $50-$100 limit,

33

which is substantially larger than what you normally even think about playing. Should you take a shot?

One thing to keep in mind is that, in general, the higher the limit is, the better the players are. Now this doesn't mean that there aren't some bad players in the very big games. But what happens, especially in a game like (Texas) hold'em, is that a few extremely good players can appear to play very loose and wild at times, yet they still are playing quite well. When you see someone playing like this at a smaller limit, most likely they do play poorly. But at the higher limits, this type of play does not necessarily mean that this person is a weak player. A few great players are able to play more hands because (1) they play very well on the later streets and are able to "make up ground," and (2) they have an extremely good line on certain opponents and are able to implement counter strategies that normally are wrong but in this case have become quite profitable. If you are unaware of this, someone who appears to be playing quite poorly just might be playing at an expert level. This means that playing in the higher-limit game, especially if your bankroll is relatively small, could be a disaster.

Trap No. 3: Failure to understand that the competition does adjust to your style of play. "I used to win pretty regularly, but now I never seem to win anymore." This statement is typical of those I hear all the time. They usually come from relatively new players who learned to play fairly tight and originally got more than their fair share of action, meaning that they did well. But what happens is that your regular opponents learn to adjust. For example, even poor players learn not to call someone who virtually never bluffs. At the other extreme, the very best players will play differently against many of their opponents, especially if they can isolate them. Unless you also can develop some of these skills, you essentially will be what is known as a "weak tight" player. This type of player will win at the smaller limits where the competition is not too tough, but he tends to do poorly once his opponents have adjusted to his style of play.

Another interesting thing is that the top players prefer to play against weak tight opponents rather than against wild reckless ones. This is because it is fairly easy to know exactly where you are against someone who just plays tight but with little skill. Ironically, weak tight players do win money from wild reckless ones, but they may do even worse against experts than poor players who also happen to be very unpredictable.

Throwing Money

I have been told many times that if you play poker well, "your opponents will throw money at you." I've heard this from extremely good players, world-class players, not-so-good players, and broke players standing on the rail. Are they right? Is it possible to get other players to throw their chips your way? Or is this just more of the same silliness you often hear in the poker world?

I have slowly become convinced that the above statement is true but not exactly accurate. I believe that if you play very well, *your opponents will not take their fair share*. In essence, they *are* throwing their money at you. They mainly do it by allowing you either to save bets or to win more pots than you would have the right to win if they actually knew what your cards were. For instance, weak players will give you too many free cards and will not raise you very often. This includes many times when their hands clearly warrant a raise. In fact, a great deal of the expert's profit will come from the failure of some of his opponents to take their fair share.

Here is an example. You are playing middle-limit seven-card stud. You have a queen high three flush with the queen up. You raise, hoping to steal the antes, but get called in two places. On fourth street, you catch an off-suit four. Since none of your opponents caught anything threatening, you bet again, and (as expected) both of your opponents call. Now on fifth street, you catch another off-suit four, bet, and win the pot.

Why did you win the pot? The answer is easy. You caught enough to scare your two opponents out. If they knew that in reality you had only a measly pair of fours and a three-flush, you would have been "bombarded with chips" and probably would have lost the pot. But in my opinion, if you play well, it's not that hard to take advantage of scare cards. The reason for this is that you will be playing in a tight but aggressive style, which means that your weaker-playing opponents will expect you to have a better hand than you often have. In addition, they will be scared if they think it is even remotely possible that you have a cinch hand.

The best players I know win a great deal of money by stealing more than their fair share of pots. They do this by getting the weaker players to release hands that they would never fold if they knew what the good players really had. In addition, as already mentioned, the best players get more than their share of free cards, which also allows them to win some pots that they don't deserve.

However, I am convinced that just playing technically correct, especially at the higher limits, is not enough to allow you to manipulate your weaker-playing opponents in this manner. You also must project a positive attitude and be very sure of yourself. The most successful players I know seem to possess a quiet confidence.

At the other extreme are those players who constantly complain about how bad they are running. I don't know of any players like this who are successful. At least this is true of those players at the middle and higher limits. Perhaps the complainers are unsuccessful because they just don't play that well, or because their constant griping actually inspires some of their weak-playing opponents to play better. Or maybe it is a combination of the two. In any case, these people seem to be consistent losers.

Think about it! Think about the players you know who constantly complain about how bad they are running or how unlucky they always are. Do any of them win consistently? I suspect that the answer in almost all cases will be no. When I am running bad, which certainly happens, I try not to let many people know about it. I believe this is the best policy.

Again, let me emphasize that I think quiet confidence is the way to poker success. However, there is a lot more to it than that. You also need to play very well. But once you become a good player the confidence you need should come easily.

Why You Lose

In my opinion, there are three basic reasons why typical players lose. Although it's not easy to overcome these problems, a good understanding of them will lead you in the right direction.

Reason No. 1: Going on tilt. Most of us have experienced "going on tilt" or "steaming" at one time or another. A reasonable definition of going on tilt is to play badly because you are frustrated by your recent results. Usually this translates into playing too many hands, but it also can mean playing too aggressively or not letting go of a hand that clearly has too small a chance to win to be profitable. The desire to "get even" can prove costly to many players.

I believe the way to control going on tilt is to understand that the short-term luck factor in almost all forms of poker is quite large in relation to the size of the bets. This means that even if you are playing at an expert level, which very few people are capable of doing, a reasonable possibility still exists that after a short period of time, you can be significantly behind. In fact, the short-term luck factor is so large that it is possible for these unlucky short periods of time to actually last for a fairly long time, such as several months or even longer in some forms of poker.

Understanding this fact alone will help many people play their best most of the time. When you are running bad, it does not mean that you are the unluckiest person in the world. Even the best of players expect to have a bad streak every now and then. But if you also begin to play poorly, you should expect to lose in the long run.

Reason No. 2: Flawed basic strategy. If you do not understand what correct play is, do not expect to be successful. For example, in seven-card stud, if you always play middle pairs on third street — even if your cards are dead — don't expect to be a winning player.

Basic strategy is really a poor term, because it is actually quite complicated in most forms of poker. You need to consider not only the hand you are holding, but also what the other players have done, how the other players perceive you, your position in the betting action, how loose or tight your opponents play, and many other things. If you often find yourself in situations where you are uncertain as to the right course of action, your basic strategy probably needs some more work.

Reason No. 3: Poor Judgment. Here's an example from hold'em. Suppose someone limps in from middle position, and you are in late position with:

Obviously you are going to play, but should you raise or just call. The answer to this of course is found in your basic strategy. If your basic strategy says to be more inclined to raise if you have good control over this person, if the remaining players to act are tight, if the remaining players are unlikely to play back with funny hands, etc. and otherwise to just call, then you are on the right track. But observe that to make these evaluations correctly requires good judgment, and these types of decisions come up all the time in poker, especially in complex games like hold'em and seven-card stud.

One thing I have noticed is that the very best players have superior judgment. In fact, I believe superior judgment can make up for a basic strategy that is a little faulty. (It will not make up for a basic strategy that is severely flawed.) But it can take a long time to develop this skill to a high degree.

So how do you develop superior judgment? The answer goes back to the usual things I often talk about. Developing good judgment requires, among other things, a lot of experience, a lot of thinking about the game, and being able to talk things over with someone who you know is an expert player. By the way, while many players claim to be experts; very few are.

Finally, superior judgement requires a logical thinking process. Those of you who base many of your decisions on emotion or instinct, do not stand much of a chance.

Afterthought

General Concepts

I consider the most important essay in this section to be the one titled "Poker Magic." The reason is that to be a winning player, you must play extremely well. If this is the case, you can, and probably will, win a lot of money. On the other hand, if you play only fairly well, you might win some money, but you won't win a lot. And if you venture into the higher limits, where the games are much tougher, you probably will be a big loser.

I know many players who do certain things well or who put a great deal of emphasis on a small number of ideas or concepts. Although these ideas have their place in a poker game they are not enough to make someone into a winning player. For example, being skilled at picking up tells will help you win a little more if you already play well. But you still will be a loser if most of your basic strategy is badly flawed, no matter how well you read your opponents. Needless to say, these people usually are broke or near broke most of the time, and they never come close to achieving the success that others seem to achieve.

Poker is not an easy game. To a novice player, its subtleties and complexities are hidden. To many others who play regularly, this is also true. In fact, only a very small number of people really excel at the game of poker. But with the right amount of work and study, coupled with a great deal of playing experience, it can be done.

Part Two
Technical Ideas

Technical Ideas

Introduction

One area of poker that I consider of utmost importance is what I refer to as "technical ideas." Needless to say, this domain has to do with the mathematics that govern the play of the game. But it is much broader than most people think. Technical ideas range from things like the mathematical value of your hand to the mathematics that determine the amount of chips you should have.

Many beginning players think this is all there is to poker. Other players, those less mathematically inclined, usually dismiss this topic and declare that "poker is a people game." My attitude incorporates some of both ideas. Again, poker is very complex, and to be really successful at the game you must have a deep understanding of all aspects of it. If you overemphasize the technical ideas, I suspect that you won't do very well as a player. On the other hand, if you chose to ignore them, your results also will be disappointing.

Mathematical Winners

In some of my other writings, I have touched on a subject that I think deserves more attention. It is the idea of mathematical players, also known as the "new breed," versus the (old time) instinct players. In the past, perhaps just 10 to 15 years ago, all the best players probably would have fit into the instinct category. These people learned their trade over many years, slowly became pretty good players, and did win significant amounts of money.

But then something dramatic happened. A new type of player began to appear on the scene. This new breed approached the game in a much more scientific manner and began to accumulate the chips. The old-time instinct players never really had a chance.

The best example I know of this new type of thinking appears in David Sklansky's *The Theory of Poker*, which originally appeared under the title of *Sklansky on Poker Theory*. There, much of the game of poker is quantified in a scientific and mathematical manner. Those who do not study this book, perhaps the most important poker book ever written, will simply be left behind by those who do.

However, there is a great misconception among non-mathematical players as to what this powerful winning approach is like. It is not "knowing the odds better." I constantly hear remarks similar to "he knows the percentages better than anyone," or "players like you may know the percentages, but there is a lot more to poker than just knowing the percentages."

Of course, this is true. Anyone who plays poker for a reasonable period of time should have a good enough "feel" for the basic odds and appropriate percentages to do just about as well as someone who knows the exact "numbers" in every situation. So what exactly is the mathematical approach? Is it something that only a few mathematically inclined players can execute? Is it an approach that is too abstract to even write about? Or is it something else? Let me see if I can answer by an example.

Suppose all the cards are out in a heads-up pot. Your opponent bets, and you are trying to determine whether to call but you can only beat a bluff. The instinct player might consider that there is some chance his opponent is bluffing but he still will not really know what to do. The mathematical player will try to attach a probability to the chance that his opponent is bluffing, compare this probability to the size of the pot versus the bet size, and then make a decision. Specifically, you may decide that an opponent would bluff 10 percent of the time in this situation meaning that if the pot is offering you more than 9-to-1, a call is correct.

Notice that good judgment is still required for the mathematical player. Continuing with the above example, if your opponent actually would bluff much more than 10 percent of the time, then the mathematical player would be laying down too many hands. Also, the mathematical player will consider things like tells, betting information, and playing patterns to adjust his probabilities.

This is just one example of the things that the new breed will do. Other things include playing in such a manner as to manipulate his opponent into either bluffing too much or not at all. An example of this from ace-to-five lowball would be to call from the big blind with:

and then to check and call after the draw. After his opponents see this, they would be less likely to bluff him in a similar spot. Of course, he later might be holding something like a rough 10 and have no intention of calling any bet. However, if the bet does come, it is less likely that his opponent, especially if he is fairly observant, is bluffing.

So what's the bottom line? It is simply that today's young, modern, scientific player plays much better than his older counterpart. It is true that the games are tougher, but today's experts are better than ever and still win more than their share of money. Put another way, if your approach to playing poker is not similar to that just described, it is unlikely that you will amount to more than a marginal winner at the poker table.

Of course, poker is much more complicated than these examples show. However, this type of approach can be applied to almost all aspects of the game. If you are not attempting to do this, you will have trouble keeping up with those who do.

Computerized Hold'em?

Warning! Hold'em computer simulations can be very inaccurate.

There are now several books out on the game of Texas hold'em that are based on computer simulations. Also, numerous articles recently have been printed (and they continue to appear) on hold'em that are based on this approach. Although much of this material is quite interesting, and I think the authors are well-intentioned, most of the advice given will cost the reader a great deal of money.

The reason is that hold'em is not played at all like most of the recently published computer simulations assume, even though I am sure that a lot of programming effort (by the appropriate authors) was put into this work.

Let me be specific. The typical computer analysis assumes that one player has some specific hand, he is up against a certain number of opponents who each hold two random cards, all hands are played through the river, and the best hand wins in a showdown. Of course, no hold'em game is played like this, even though the actions of an occasional weak player will approach this horrendous strategy. In addition, drawing conclusions about how to play hold'em based on this type of simulation can be extremely expensive.

So what does this type of computer simulation show? It indicates that you can profitably play hands like king-three offsuit in many handed pots, that there are lots of set-over-set confrontations, that big pairs are not worth as much as most experts think, and that you should virtually never throw a hand away when you are in the blind position, just to name a few misconceptions.

The problem with this type of computer simulation is that the programmers, even though they may have worked very hard on their programs, have not programmed any realistic strategy. There are probably two reasons for this. First, hold'em strategy may not be well understood by the appropriate authors; second, and most important, programming accurate strategy would be a gigantic task. To prove my point, suppose you are playing in a typical Las Vegas $10-$20 or $20-$40 game. If a player raises before the flop, it usually means that his hand is much stronger than it would be if he just called before the flop. Consequently, the programmer should use a different range of hands for when there is a raise than he uses for when there is only a call. But some players occasionally do call with very strong hands, such as two aces. This means that the programmer also should allocate a small probability to the calling hands, making them extremely powerful.

In addition, the programmer needs to account for differences between legitimate raises and possible steal raises. Legitimate raises usually occur in an early position or when other players have already entered the pot. These raises tell the other players that they are probably, but not absolutely, looking at a reasonably strong hand (and many opponents now will adjust the range of hands they will play). Possible steal raises, which occur when a player is the first one in from a late position, usually mean that the raiser is playing a wider range of hands since he has a decent chance of picking up the blinds. (By the way, I have seen several strategies supposedly based on computer simulations that do not take into account the difference between a legitimate raise and a steal raise. Needless to say, this is a very serious error.)

As you can see, I have only scratched the surface. There is a lot more to just before-the-flop raising than I have discussed. As for the rest of the game, things quickly get much more complicated. The computer simulations that I've seen do not include things like semi-bluffing, betting for value, betting to stop free cards, raising to gain free cards, slowplaying, check-raising, taking into account the size of the pot when either calling or folding, manipulating the size of the pot so that your opponent will misplay his hand when a certain type of flops hit, how certain opponents react to scare cards, and much more.

So what's the bottom line? It is this: There is probably something to learn from this material, but don't spend much time studying it and don't put your bankroll behind this type of advice. It can and probably will be very expensive.

What's My Frequency?

I have recently read several articles on frequency counts. The idea is to monitor your opponents, count the number of hands they play in some given period of time — usually an hour — and from these counts, quickly determine who the tight and loose players are, which of course affects your strategy. Sounds pretty good, doesn't it? Just a quick count, and you not only have a good line on your opponents but also are on your way to huge wins! Unfortunately, I don't believe these frequency counts are very accurate. Let's discuss why.

Suppose you are in a (typical?) poker game where the average number of hands dealt in an hour is 45. Also suppose one of your opponents plays an average of 10 hands per hour. Does this mean that after an hour, your frequency count for this player will be exactly 10? *Most likely not!* The reason is that 10 is only the *expected* number of hands this player will play. In reality, he might play a different number. If he gets a good run of cards, then this opponent may play many more than 10 hands. But if the cards run bad, he might play significantly fewer hands.

(In addition, the number of hands he plays probably will be affected by the action of his opponents. Specifically, if the game is very passive, he may play some extra hands. If the game is very aggressive, he probably will be raised out of some pots, thus playing a fewer number of hands. However, for the purpose of this analysis, this effect will be ignored.)

Let's get a little technical. There is something in the world of statistics called the Binomial Theorem that will allow us to calculate the probability of the different number of hands our 10-hand-per-hour player will play. I'm not going to explain the Binomial Theorem here, but the following table provides the appropriate results. The second column in the table is most important as it gives the cumulative probability of playing that given number of hands or fewer.

Probability of Playing Different Number of Hands
When 10 Out of 45 Hands are Expected to be Played

No	Prob	Cum Prob	No	Prob	Cum
0	.----	.----	11	.1418	.7129
1	.0002	.0002	12	.1043	.8172
2	.0010	.0012	13	.0756	.8928
3	.0041	.0053	14	.0494	.9422
4	.0122	.0175	15	.0292	.9714
5	.0285	.0460	16	.0156	.9870
6	.0544	.1004	17	.0076	.9946
7	.0865	.1869	18	.0034	.9980
8	.1174	.3043	19	.0014	.9994
9	.1379	.4422	20	.0005	.9999
10	.1418	.5840	20+	.0001	1.0000

Now let's notice an interesting fact. Approximately 99 percent of the playable-hand probability distribution is from three hands per hour through 17 hands per hour. Also, remember that this is the same person. Consequently, it would be possible to get a very low number when counting the hands he plays in one particular hour and a very high number in another hour. So what good is a frequency count?

In my opinion, the statistical spread of hands that is highly likely is just too great to make this type of table analysis very meaningful. In addition, it can be especially dangerous for someone new to poker, who does not (as yet) have the ability to quickly realize that some of his first impressions may be wrong. And sticking with these first impressions can prove to be very expensive.

Instead of counting the number of hands an opponent plays, I suggest you watch the cards that get turned up when a hand is over. For example, when playing hold'em, if one of your opponents turns up a 9-6 suited when in an early position, he is probably playing loose. However, beware of the expert player who occasionally will play a hand like this just to throw his opponents off.

Some Comments
on Fluctuations

One thing I show — and mathematically quantify — in
Gambling Theory and Other Topics is that winning players can and
do have significant losing streaks. Does this mean that if you have
a significant losing streak, you are a winning player? I suppose that
some readers will make that conclusion, but keep in mind that all
other factors being equal, a losing player is much more likely to
have a significant loss than a winning player.

But are all other factors usually equal? Actually, they are almost
never equal. In fact, in many situations, a great player is more likely
to go broke than a good player. (This has to do with the fact that
those strategies that produce a slightly higher win rate are usually
accompanied by much more risk.) Also, as I state in the above-
mentioned book, the bad players, as long as they keep playing, will
always go broke. This is absolutely true despite whatever silly
money-management schemes they may adopt.

Changing the subject slightly, we all should realize that the large
fluctuations present in all forms of poker are really the skilled
player's friend. The large standard deviation that allows the weak
player to sometimes (much too often?) draw out is the hook that
keeps him playing. In fact, instead of bouncing the cards off the
dealer's head when the live one hits the gut straight against you, be
happy in the knowledge that this is the type of play that causes these
players to deplete their bankrolls in the long run.

Another thing an expert player should be conscious of is that
Texas hold'em requires a smaller bankroll than seven-card stud.
(Actually high draw, jacks or better to open, and Omaha eight or
better both require smaller bankrolls than hold'em for the expert.
Unfortunately, high draw, thanks to the changed laws in California,
has just about died out, and Omaha eight or better is not that
popular and is spread only in a few cardrooms.) This is because the
ratio of the expectation to the standard deviation is more positive in

hold'em.[1] Again, keep in mind that this statement is true only for the highly skilled expert player (and, of course, the competition must be considered). On the other hand, if you are a marginal player, your bankroll requirements — which are now much larger — are roughly the same in Texas hold'em, lowball, and razz (that is, razz played with a small to medium ante). This is because the real experts at hold'em can win at a higher rate than the experts in the other games. (Bankroll requirements in seven-card stud are even larger at the higher limits, because the ante is proportionately much larger.)

By the way, the bankroll swings present in all forms of limit poker can be extremely frustrating. Many players, who otherwise play reasonably well, cannot handle running bad and incur significant loses because they go on tilt.

Perhaps even more devastating are positive swings for a losing player. Now, the best player in Las Vegas or wherever — and I have met many of these — will see his bankroll disappear as he moves up and challenges even stronger competition. No wonder so many self-proclaimed, world-class players are currently broke.

Another thing to realize is that an expert player does not walk into a cardroom, play for a while, and then leave with everyone's money. It's true that he will have an occasional night when he scores a huge win, but he also will have some losing nights. However, in the long run, he does expect to be ahead. But as I show in *Gambling Theory and Other Topics*, this long run in some forms of poker can take a *very* long time to appear.

Finally, keep in mind that the game you play will change over time. Your opponents may begin to adjust to your style of play; loose, losing players may begin to play tighter; new players may show up whose style of play interferes with yours; and so forth. This means that your opinion of how well you should be doing may not be as accurate as you think.

---

[1]This is not true anymore in limit games where a lot of bets are put in on the opening round.

What You Can Make Playing Poker

How much can a good player make playing poker? What about a great player? What if you just play OK? These are important questions for some of you, especially if you are considering playing poker seriously.

Following are some tables that illustrate how a player in each of the three categories just mentioned should expect to do per hour of play. I want to point out that these numbers are subjective, and in some cases, they could be significantly off. (Also keep in mind that any individual hour could be much different.) In addition these figures are based on my experience of the games in Las Vegas and in Los Angeles, especially those games at the Horseshoe, the Mirage, the Bicycle Club, and the Commerce Club.

Table I: Texas Hold'em

Limit	Player		
	OK	Good	Great
$3-$6	$4	$8	$12
$4-$8	5	10	14
$10-$20	10	20	35
$20-$40	10	25	50
$30-$60	10	25	65
$50-$100	5	30	80

Table II: Seven Card Stud

Limit	Player		
	OK	Good	Great
$1-$5	$3	$5	$8
$5-$10	7	10	15
$10-$20	10	20	30
$15-$30	10	20	40
$30-$60	15	30	70
$50-$100	10	35	90
$75-$150	15	65	115

Table III: Razz

Limit	Player		
	OK	Good	Great
$15-$30	$20	$20	$30
$30-$60	30	30	60

Table IV: Lowball Draw (Ace-to-Five)

Limit	Player		
	OK	Good	Great
$3-$6	$5	$10	$12
$5-$10	7	12	15
$15-$30	15	25	40
$30-$60	20	35	50
$75-$150	60	90	135

Table V: Omaha — Eight or Better

Limit	Player		
	OK	Good	Great
$3-$6	$5	$10	$15
$10-$20	10	25	35

There are a few things you should notice. First, the games in general definitely get tougher as the stakes get bigger, meaning that the relative win rate for the better players goes down.

Second, my estimated win rates probably are not as high as some people claim to do. I suspect these individuals overestimate their abilities because they do not realize that they have run better than expected.

Third, you need to realize that your rating as a player — that is, OK, good, or great — has a lot to do with the stakes you are playing at. Specifically, since the games in general get tougher as you move up, someone who might be considered good (or even great) at a low limit may discover that winning at a high limit is very difficult.

And finally, these figures are supposed to represent typical games on typical days. There are times, such as during the major tournaments, when much better games can be found. When this is the case, expect better win rates. By the way, the opposite is also true. If you are not game selective, expect to do worse than my estimates.

Bankroll Requirements: Another Look

One of the things I show in *Gambling Theory and Other Topics* is how to estimate bankroll requirements for different poker games. By using two parameters, your win rate (WR) and your standard deviation (σ) (where the standard deviation is the statistical measure of fluctuations or short-term luck that is present in a poker game), I derive the following equation, which is an estimate of your required bankroll (BR) to ensure survival.

$$BR = \frac{9\sigma^2}{4(WR)}$$

This equation assumes that three standard deviations below the mean is the worst you can possibly have at any time and that you plan to play one particular game for life. (For those of you who have read *Gambling Theory and Other Topics*, even though this equation does not appear in the same form, it is exactly equivalent to the final equation that appears in my book.)

For example, if you are a fairly tight $10-$20 hold'em player and play in typical Las Vegas games, your standard deviation should be about $200 per hour. This means that if your win rate is approximately $20 per hour, your required bankroll to ensure survival is approximately $4,500.

$$4,500 = \frac{(9)(200)^2}{(4)(20)}$$

If your win rate for the same game is $10 per hour, this equation estimates a required bankroll of $9,000; if your win rate is $30 per hour, the estimate of your required bankroll is now $3,000. Also, if you play seven-card stud, your standard deviation for that game is 20 percent to 80 percent larger, depending on the limit.[2] Consequently, to ensure survival, your required bankroll may be as much as three times larger or even more for each appropriate win rate. (The larger stud games have the higher standard deviation, not only because most players play faster as the stakes get bigger, but also because the ante is proportionately larger at the higher limits.) Finally, lowball players will have approximately the same bankroll requirements as hold'em players (for an appropriate win rate), providing they play in a game that allows pots to be killed.

However, you won't have the same win rate and same standard deviation every time you play. Depending on the game, sometimes these parameters are larger, and sometimes they are smaller. This is known as a non-self-weighting effect that statistically reduces your sample size. In plain English, this means that my equation actually gives an underestimate of your required bankroll. To be safe, I recommend that you increase the computed estimate by 10 percent.

Bankroll requirements as well as estimates of the standard deviation for different poker games and a usable formula for computing your standard deviation are discussed in detail in *Gambling Theory and Other Topics*, which is must reading for all serious players. But I recently have come to believe that the equation I've used to determine one's required bankroll, even with the 10 percent adjustment, may still underestimate what is required to survive. The reason for this is that even though it is possible to have more than three standard deviations at some particular time, the path of results that lead to this value may have been lower at some previous point. In my way of approximating the "lower limit equation," this possibility did not exist.

---

[2] As mentioned previously, this is not true anymore in some hold'em games where a great deal of money is going into the pot early.

Ironically, part of the reason that I originally published this material was to show how much more money is required to ensure survival than what most people think. Now I am convinced that even these estimates are still too low.

One final thought: These numbers and the equation assume that you are planning to play some particular game for life. If you are just "taking a shot," you can make do with much less. However, *if you do lose, make sure that you quickly move back to a lower limit. If you don't, you can easily be wiped out, even if you have an expected "earn" in the game.*

What Your Bankroll Should Be

Earlier I gave estimates for what different winning players should be able to average in different poker games at many different limits. Unfortunately, even though you might expect to make some particular amount for any given hour played, you will not always make exactly that amount. Moreover you might even lose.

Even the best players will have lots of losing hours and, in fact, occasionally have prolonged losing streaks. This is because the standard deviation, the statistical measure of short-term luck, is very large when compared to one's expected win over a small period of time. Consequently, the next logical question to ask is, "How much do I need to ensure survival?"

What follows are my estimates of the required bankroll to ensure survival for someone who plays either OK, good, or great for the particular game and limit below. (For a more thorough explanation of how I came up with these numbers, see *Gambling Theory and Other Topics.*)

Table I: Texas Hold'em

Limit	Player		
	OK	Good	Great
$3-$6	$1,500	$1,100	$1,000
$4-$8	2,800	1,800	1,700
$10-$20	8,000	4,900	3,900
$20-$40	39,600	20,000	11,200
$30-$60	59,400	37,600	19,900
$50-$100	165,000	74,900	38,700

Table II: Seven Card Stud

Limit	Player		
	OK	Good	Great
$1-$5	$750	$600	$500
$5-$10	2,000	1,800	1,500
$10-$20	5,600	3,200	2,500
$15-$30	15,500	9,400	5,600
$30-$60	92,800	52,800	24,000
$50-$100	260,000	132,000	68,000
$75-$150	437,000	167,000	97,000

Table III: Razz

Limit	Player		
	OK	Good	Great
$15-$30	$4,900	$4,800	$4,100
$30-$60	25,500	24,200	16,100

Table IV: Lowball Draw (Ace-to-Five)

Limit	Player		
	OK	Good	Great
$3-$6	$600	$300	$350
$5-$10	1,500	1,000	900
$15-$30	6,600	5,000	3,900
$30-$60	40,900	25,500	20,900
$75-$150	75,200	53,900	41,200

Table V: Omaha — Eight or Better

Limit	Player		
	OK	Good	Great
$3-$6 $10-$20	$600 2,500	$300 1,500	$200 1,300

Again, there are a few things you should notice. First, the higher your win rate is, the smaller your bankroll needs to be. I won't explain in this short space why this is so, but it should be intuitively obvious to most people.

Second, notice how large the bankroll requirement is for the big stud games. This has to do not only with the players playing very fast in these games, but also with the progressively larger ante structure. Put another way, large limit seven-card stud is a highly fluctuating game, and if you plan on playing it, be prepared for a roller coaster ride.

Third, you need to realize that your rating as a player — that is OK, good, or great — has a lot to do with the stakes that you are playing at. Specifically, since the games in general get tougher as you move up, someone who might be considered good (or even great) at a low limit may discover that winning at a high limit is very difficult.

Fourth, these figures are supposed to represent typical games on typical days. There are times, such as during the major tournaments, when much better games can be found. When this is the case, expect better win rates, which mean lower bankroll requirements (for those games). On the other hand, if you are not game selective, you may need even more money to ensure survival than these estimates indicate.

And finally, these tables assume that you are planning to play a particular game for life. If you are willing to step down after a couple of losses, you can make do with a much smaller sum.

The Quickest Way to Go Broke

I occasionally see advice that is the equivalent of overbetting your bankroll. For example, the following statement recently appeared in another writer's poker column: "The quickest way to build a bankroll is to set a loss limit and pyramid your winnings up to higher limits." Is this correct? Is pyramiding with a loss limit the sure path to riches? Or is this just another piece of silly advice that constantly appears in the gambling literature?

In *Gambling Theory and Other Topics*, I point out that you would like to balance your expectation and standard deviation (the short-term measurement of luck) against your bankroll. The thing to keep in mind is that the larger your bankroll, the larger the fluctuations you can withstand. As I say in my book, *"This leads to the conclusion that there is always some best game for you to be playing in."* Obviously, pyramiding usually puts you in a game that is not even close to what is the best game for you. This invites disaster. Here's another quote from my theory book:

Again, I want to emphasize how important this idea is. It may be the most significant gambling concept that I will ever write about. Simply put, *there are some people out there who don't make what they should because they constantly play in games too small for their bankrolls, and there are some people out there who also don't make what they should simply because they constantly play in games that are too big for their bankrolls,* even though they have the ability for a positive "earn." Don't let this happen to you!

Now I'm not against occasionally taking a shot. I have done this sort of thing many times myself. Just be aware that if your shot fails, you must be ready to quickly move to a smaller game.

Clearly, pyramiding is not the quickest way to build a bankroll. In fact, it is probably one of the quickest ways to destroy your bankroll, even though you always may be playing in a game where you definitely have the best of it.

Setting a loss limit, sometimes called a stop loss, is also just plain wrong. Suppose you are in a game and are a big favorite, but you have just lost a pot. Are you now supposed to quit because your losses have gone over some silly artificial number? Of course not! In general, you should continue to play a game as long as you expect to do well in it. But remember, expecting to do well does not guarantee success. The standard deviation in most forms of poker is just too big in the short run for this to be true.

There are also lots of legitimate reasons to quit a game. One of them is because your losses have become so great that your expectation and standard deviation are no longer well balanced against your bankroll. In plain English, the stakes have become too large for the amount of money you have; that is, your risk of going broke, even though you may be an expert player, is now just too great.

Returning to the idea of pyramiding, I know about half a dozen poker players who actually play quite well but who keep themselves broke. The reason for this is that whenever these people get a win, they immediately go to a larger game and continue this process. Eventually, they play in a game large enough that when they run bad, which will inevitably happen, they find themselves back in the small limits or on the rail looking for a stake.

So when is it right to go to a larger game? In general, you want your bankroll to increase at least in the same proportion as the betting limits increase. For example, suppose you are a $10-$20 player and you have settled on a bankroll of $3,500 to play at this limit. If your bankroll begins to approach $7,000, consider playing the $20-$40 game. (In reality, you may want your bankroll to grow even larger. This is because there are more experts at the higher limit, meaning that your relative win rate will probably be smaller. In addition, the larger games tend to be played faster, which means they have a larger standard deviation.) Similarly, if your bankroll drops below $2,000 dollars, $5-$10 is probably your best game. This is true, even if you are the best poker player in the world.

The Magic Number

One question I am occasionally asked by other players is, "How much should I buyin for." It seems as if some people are looking for a magic number of chips to purchase. Well, is there a magic number? Is a certain number of chips clearly more profitable than another number? And how do we determine the correct amount?

Before answering these questions, let me state that I think there *is* an optimal amount to buy in for. Let's see if I am right.

Suppose you were playing $15-$30 razz with a $1 ante, and further suppose that you were able to buy in for only $1. Well, you wouldn't be able to do anything creative, you would be eligible to win only the antes, and if you had a good hand, you wouldn't be able to defend it or to extract any chips from your opponents. But there is one advantage that you would have: You would be able to play every hand to the end and, as just pointed out, be eligible to win the antes in a showdown.

But how often would you win the antes in a showdown? I'm not really sure, but I suspect that about one out of three times is in the ballpark, assuming that you are against typical opponents. This means that in a full game of eight players, you would show a profit of $5 for every three hands you played. If you then could leave the table, cash in your $5 profit, buy in again for only $1, and continue this process, in a typical hour's worth of play — which means about 40 hands — your expectation would be slightly more than $65 dollars per hour. Not bad. (If the game was short-handed, your expectation per hour probably would be even higher, since you would win a higher percentage of the pots and there would be more hands per hour. I'm sure this would more than balance the fact that the pots you do win would now be smaller since there are fewer antes.) I don't know anyone, who is capable of winning at this high a rate in $15-$30 razz. In fact, I don't think anyone even comes close. So it sure seems like a $1 buy-in is the magic number.

However, there is one problem: No cardroom will allow you to buy in for only $1, much less to leave the table every third hand (on average), cash in your expected $5 profit, then return to make another buy-in. A few rooms permit one short buy-in after you have gone broke. But even these rooms require you to then make a "full" buy-in after your short buy-in if you lose all your chips.

So even though it looks like $1 (or one chip) is the ultimate buy-in, it won't do you any good to know this. I suspect there may be some advantages to always making the minimal buy-in, but ironically, I have always done just the opposite. I am of the school that believes a lot of chips in front of you makes your opponents — at least some of them — think you are a significant winner. This, in turn, causes them to play less aggressively against you and perhaps to make errors against you that they normally would not make. In other words, they may be intimidated and miss a bet, or even better, they won't bluff you out of a pot in a situation where they easily can do so.

But this razz example seems to indicate that there are advantages to going all in. What are they? Basically, when it doesn't cost much, certain weak hands become correct to play, even in situations where you know they will win only occasionally. For instance, in high games, hands like inside-straight draws, small pairs, three-flushes with two cards to come, and even just one overcard can all become profitable plays if you have to put in only a fraction of a real bet. On the low side, two-card draws and draws to rough hands also can be winning plays.

So what's the conclusion in the real world, where the minimum buy-in rule does exist? Well, I'm not really sure. But I think I'll stick to my big buy-in philosophy, although buying in for the minimum does have some things to offer.

Win Rate Accuracy Revisited

I recently read that you can play hundreds of hours and still not have enough time accumulated to really have a good handle on your win rate. I believe this is true. In fact, I suspect that most of you who have many years of experience playing poker will agree.

In *Gambling Theory and Other Topics*, I show that the standard deviation — the statistical measurement of "luck" that I often talk about — is usually so large (in the short term) compared to your expectation that in most forms of poker, you will need to play for an extremely long time to get an accurate handle on your actual win rate. This is true even if you are a highly skilled player, and it is especially true in the larger games, where the fluctuations are relatively much larger than in the smaller games.

But there is another side to this story. Sometimes you don't need to log that many hours to have a good feel for how you should do in a game. In fact you often can get a good idea of what your win rate should be by taking into account the other players who are sitting at the table with you.

Here's what I mean. First, if you regularly play in games with a lot of professional players, don't expect to have a high win rate. I don't care how well you play. On the other hand, if your game is constantly full of tourists, then you can be a significant winner.

Also take into account how the best players do. For instance, in $10-$20 hold'em, the very best players — and there are only a few in Las Vegas — average just over $35 an hour if they are selective in their games. For $15-$30 stud, the figure is about $40 an hour. This means that if you have been averaging something like $80 an hour in one of these games, don't expect it to continue.

Another thing to watch for is the type of plays that your opponents make. For example, in high draw, jacks or better to open (played with a joker) if you see a lot of people calling with shorts — that is, a pair lower than jacks — you know the game is good, and you can anticipate a high win rate. If there is a lot of sandbagging —

passing good hands from an early position with the intention of raising a late-position opener — you know the game is bad, and now you can expect a poor win rate.

Similar types of plays occur in all games. Here are a few examples. In lowball, if late-position players constantly call early-position opponents and then draw two cards, you know the game is good. On the other hand, if after the draw, many opponents are betting nines or better when they are first to act and 10s or better when they are last to act, then expect a low win rate. (Of course, I am assuming that they drew cards.)

In hold'em, if some of your opponents will call on the flop with weak hands, and there are many players still to act behind them, then the game is good. If several players are aware that it is often correct to bluff at flops that contain pairs, the game may be much tougher.

In seven-card stud, if opponents automatically play hands even if their cards are not very live, then you should be a significant winner in the game. If the opposite is true, the game could be quite tough.

As you can see, I have only scratched the surface. There is much more to what makes a poker game good or bad than the few things I have mentioned.

But if you have a good understanding of the game you are playing in and are well-disciplined, then by observation, you will gain a pretty good idea of what your win rate should be in a relatively short period of time. However, if your understanding of the game is poor, don't expect to do very well in the long run, even if your recent results are spectacular.

Finally, let me mention one last thing. If you are capable of playing well but "steam" a fair amount, don't expect your overall results to be very good. If you don't play that well and steam a fair amount, don't expect to be playing poker very long. Losing control, as many people seem prone to do, is the downfall of many otherwise successful poker players.

Inversely Correlated
Poker Games

As the weather gets hotter, more people go to the beach. This is an example of two events that are said to be positively correlated. This is because the occurrence of one of the events makes it more likely that the other event will happen. Similarly, two events are said to be inversely correlated if the occurrence of one of them makes it less likely that the other will happen. An example of inversely correlated events would be the more you exercise the less you spend on doctor bills. Let's see how these ideas affect correct poker strategy.

Suppose you are playing draw poker and are dealt a hand that contains two aces. What does this tell us about an opponent's hand? Basically, we know it is less likely that he will have aces, but his distribution of good hands to bad hands still will be about the same. For example, the fact that you hold two aces won't change the probability very much that your opponent holds a full house. Notice that we are describing a game that is just slightly correlated. In fact, most poker games are of this nature. Certainly draw, lowball, and stud are slightly correlated games.

The next question is, what is the correct strategy for slightly correlated games? It's this: Wait until you have a hand that from a probability point of view is most likely the best hand, and then extract the largest amount of money you can from your opponents. This leads to a style of play that is known as "tight but aggressive" and is, without a doubt, the correct way to play these games.

Of course, poker is a great deal more complicated than this. For example, with a four-flush in draw poker, it is usually incorrect to play aggressively until the hand is made. But in general, the idea of tight but aggressive play is correct.

Now let's look at a very different type of poker game, Texas hold'em. Suppose you start with

and an opponent starts with

Clearly, you have the better hand. But suppose the flop comes eight high. Now who has the better hand? Of course, your opponent does. But something else has happened. While your opponent's hand got better, your hand got worse. In fact, even though you had the better hand to begin with, you are now a big "dog" if you continue to contest this pot. Notice that we have described a game where players hands often become inversely correlated to each other.

The question arises as to what is the best strategy for playing this game? Or put another way, is tight but aggressive play still correct? Clearly, the idea of tight is still correct. If you have any doubt about this, just play every hand and see how long your chips last. But what about being aggressive, at least before the flop? Is this the correct approach?

There is no question that many of the top Texas hold'em players in Nevada and elsewhere use this approach. They are known to "jam" the pots and try to take control of the hand on their first two cards. Very often, after building large pots, these people are forced to stay in — even though the flop is not to their liking — until they are absolutely sure that they have no chance what so ever to win.

But is another approach to hold'em, based on the idea of inverse correlation available? Would it be correct to see the flop as cheaply as possible, no matter what you have, and continue playing only if it is to your liking? One well-known poker writer has (at times) strongly advocated this approach. His recommendation has been to get in cheaply and to become aggressive only if you survive the flop. Needless to say, when these ideas first appeared a number of years ago, they were radically different from anything the poker authorities previously had published on the game. Today these ideas still are radically different from most conventional thinking about the game.

However, the important question is whether this approach is correct. On one hand, many players have been quite successful at hold'em by being very aggressive from the start, and, just about everyone agrees that there are some situations where this is clearly correct. For example, suppose you start with a pair of queens, and two people are already in the pot when the action gets to you. There is no question that this hand should be played aggressively. First, you want to limit your opposition; second, and probably more important, unless an ace or a king appears on the flop, it most likely will be to your liking.

On the other hand, many two-card holdings will be inversely correlated, and it seems logical that this property does make Texas hold'em a wait-and-see game. (Limit Omaha hold'em would be even more likely a wait-and-see game, since it is seldom possible to steal the blinds.) Consequently, it appears that this strategy is on the money. *But I strongly disagree with it, and as it turns out, there is another way to approach this problem.*

What happens in hold'em is that unlike other poker games, you start with a very incomplete hand. In a sense, your first-round bet is somewhat equivalent to an ante, except that if you want to play, you have an option as to how big you would like this ante to be.

Specifically, suppose you have the same 8♠ 7♠ mentioned earlier. Most of the value this hand has occurs if you get lucky on the flop. In other words, it is a hand of "implied odds." This means that in most cases you want to play for as cheaply as possible. Compare this hand to the A♥ K♣. The A♥ K♣ clearly has value before the flop and does not require the degree of luck on the flop as the 8♠ 7♠ does. Consequently, the A♣ K♣ usually plays best with a large pre-flop ante. Even more important, you do not want to let the drawing hands in cheaply, giving them good implied odds, *so just calling before the flop with this hand is usually a mistake.*

I know almost all of the most successful limit hold'em players in Las Vegas, and every one of them is aggressive before the flop. In fact, in my opinion, a few of them are probably too aggressive. But I don't know of any successful players who consistently try to see the flop cheaply on most of their playable hands. This is just not a winning strategy.

Differences Between Stud and Hold'em

Several years back, in one of the major cardrooms in Nevada, I overheard this conversation between a tourist and a floorman. "I just won $10,000 at keno, and I know poker," said the tourist. "But what game is this?" "This is Texas hold'em," replied the floorman. "It's a form of seven-card stud." "I know how to play stud," said the tourist, who promptly took a seat and, as expected, lost a good chunk of his keno win.

Even though hold'em and stud do look similar, the two games are vastly different. In fact, it is hard to believe that two games which look so similar can be as different as they are. Yet very few people understand this.

In my opinion, stud plays something like a poker game should play. In other words, if you think you have the best hand, you usually bet. But in hold'em, correct strategy often seems reversed from what at first appears logical. Let's discuss some of the distinct differences between these two games.

Difference No. 1: Most of your luck occurs early in hold'em, while most of your luck occurs late in stud. In hold'em, your second bet is associated with seeing three new cards, but in stud, you get to see only one new card at a time. This means that there is a large element of luck between the first and second rounds in hold'em, while in stud, the opposite is true.

On the other hand, because of the community cards, the amount of luck in hold'em is minimized on the later streets. For example, when the board pairs, both you and your opponent add that pair to your hands (assuming that this card does not make either of you a set, or perhaps a flush). Think about all the times in stud when your pair of aces does not improve and loses to two small pair. (In

75

reality, there is more luck overall in stud than in hold'em.[3] This is especially true at the higher limits where the ante structure is relatively large. However, this is not true on the early streets.)

Difference No. 2: Kickers are more crucial in hold'em. In both hold'em and stud, kickers play an important role, but they are much more crucial in hold'em. For example, it is quite common in hold'em for two players to have the same general hand, such as two aces. The winner is usually the person with the better kicker. This means that the size of your kicker and how it relates to your other card becomes absolutely crucial in hold'em. In stud, if for example you have two aces on third street, your kicker has virtually no impact on how you play your hand. Of course, with other stud holdings — such as small pairs — what your kicker is can be critical in determining whether the hand should be played. But in general, this concept is much more important in hold'em.

Difference No. 3: You get to see your opponent's last card in hold'em. Because of the community cards in hold'em, you are able to see your opponent's last card, which also happens to be your last card. This means that the expert player is often able to save or get an extra bet on the end, or even sometimes steal the pot. For example, if you are very sure that your opponent is on a flush draw, and if the appropriate suit hits, you can just throw your hand away. In stud, you cannot do this. The size of the pot will force you to call automatically most of the time. (This is another example of why there is more luck in stud later in the hand.)

Difference No. 4: In stud you have to be concerned with how live your hand is. In *Seven-Card Stud For Advanced Players*, which I co-wrote with David Sklansky and Ray Zee, we show that it is sometimes correct to throw the best hand away. This would be when both of your pair cards are dead and one of your kickers is

---

[3]This is not true anymore in some limit hold'em games where a great deal of money goes into the pot before the flop.

also out. This idea is of paramount importance to winning stud play. In hold'em, since all the private cards are dealt face down, whether your hand is live or not is a concept that plays virtually no role. Consequently, stud is much more tiring to play, since you must be aware of the cards that are out, especially on third street, and how these cards impact the strength of your own hand. In hold'em, it seems that there are times when you don't need to pay any attention to what is going on. This is virtually never true in stud.

Difference No. 5: You need to check-raise more in hold'em. One of the problems with limit hold'em is that the bet on the flop can be very small when compared to the size of the pot. Consequently, a bet cannot always protect your hand, which means that it is often correct to try for a check-raise if you are in an early position and there are several players to act behind you. This is especially true if you think it is likely that the first bet will come from a late position.

In stud, the situation is often very different. Large multiway pots are not as common. Part of the reason for this is that the typical stud game has only eight players, while the typical hold'em game has 10 players. This means that trying for a check-raise is much less likely to be correct, even though you don't steal the pot very often on fourth street.

Difference No. 6: It is often correct to chase in stud. One of the problems with seven-card stud is that the pots quickly get very large, meaning that it is often correct to chase. Specifically, if it is correct to play your hand on third street, it is often correct to go all the way to the river, even if you are sure that you are up against a better hand. Hold'em is very different from this. Because the cards in the center of the table are shared by everyone, your chances of drawing out are much lower than they are in stud. Hold'em is not a game where a lot of chasing is correct.

Difference No. 7: You can steal more pots in hold'em. Since it is incorrect to do a lot of chasing in hold'em, and since the majority of the time the flop is not helpful to any particular hand, there will be many opportunities to steal on either the flop or a later street. The situation is not the same in stud. Even though you can do some stealing on fifth street (where the betting limits double) — and taking advantage of appropriate scare cards is absolutely crucial to winning play — it is still not the same as in hold'em. For example, stealing on fourth street in seven-card stud is, in reality, only a rare event. Compare this to stealing on the flop in hold'em.

Difference No. 8: Hold'em is much more of a positional game than stud. This should be fairly obvious to most people, since the blinds in hold'em always determine the order of the players to act on all betting rounds. In stud, the highest board determines who should act first, except on third street, when the person who has the lowest card showing is forced to enter the pot before anyone else. However, understanding the meaning of position and adjusting your play to account for it is still an important part of winning stud strategy. It is just that in hold'em, playing position correctly is even more important.

Difference No. 9: There are more maniacs at the hold'em tables. This has a lot to do with the large element of luck that occurs early in a hold'em hand. Put another way, getting a little out of line before the flop at the hold'em table is not penalized as much as getting out of line on third street in seven-card stud. This accounts for the larger number of wild players that you see at the hold'em tables and in many ways, at least for some people, makes hold'em more fun to play. By the way, playing like a maniac, no matter what the game, will not win the money. It is just that playing in this fashion in hold'em, especially before the flop, is not penalized as it is in stud.

Difference No. 10: Ante stealing is more important in stud. This has to do with the small blind structure in hold'em when compared to the antes and bring-in in stud. I am primarily referring to the bigger stud games where the antes are proportionately larger than they are in the smaller (stud) games. This is not true in hold'em. Here, with the exception of some very high-limit games, the blind structure stays relatively the same.

Difference No. 11: In stud, your most important decision is on third street; in hold'em, if you do not play well on the flop, you cannot win. In stud, someone who plays well on third street but just OK after that should still be a winner, especially if the opposition is not too tough. The same is not true in hold'em. If you don't play well on the flop and beyond, you will only break even at best. The reason is that in hold'em, your hand changes quickly between the first two cards and the flop. In stud, your hand changes much more slowly at first. In other words, the difference between two cards and five cards is much greater than the difference between three cards and four cards.

Final Comment: I'm sure there is a great deal more that can be written about the differences between stud and hold'em. But remember, these two games are very different, and few people can really claim to be an expert in both.

By the way, being an expert in both games is something you should strive for. This way, you will have many more opportunities to select good games.

Too Many Bad Players

I often hear people complaining that they don't want to play in a game with too many bad players. "You can't beat a game where no one knows how to play." "It's good to have a couple of anchors to help you know where you are at." "You never know who the live ones are." "I've had enough of no-fold'em hold'em." "Two aces never win." But are the complainers right? Is it true that the best games need a couple of tight players? Is it possible for games to get too good? A lot of people think so. Let's look at an example.

Suppose you are playing in a 10-handed hold'em game. Eight of your opponents play exactly like you, but the last player is a super live one. For purposes of this discussion, even though it is not very realistic, let's assume that the live one is expected to lose at a rate of $450 per hour. Ignoring the rake, this means that you (and all of your clones) expect to win in this game at a rate of $50 per hour.

Now suppose one of your clones leaves, and he is replaced by another player who plays equally as bad as the current live one. Does this mean that your expected win rate is doubled? (Actually, it would be more than doubled since there are now only eight good players left, instead of nine.) A lot of people probably think so, but I believe the answer is no.

The reason your win rate does not double is because there will be many pots where the live ones merely push their money back and forth to each other, while you — along with the other good players — correctly sit on the sidelines watching. Obviously, if only the live ones are in the pot, the good players will not expect to profit on these hands. (Also, the game may now play at a slower pace, which costs you money. For purposes of this discussion, however, I am ignoring this effect.)

This implies that every time you add a live one to your game, your expected return is diminished. I suspect that in the example just given instead of your win rate increasing to $100 per hour or more, it would now be something like $75 or $80 per hour. I also suspect that after four or five live ones are in your game, adding more terrible players would increase your win rate very little, if at all. But I don't think your win rate would drop, as long as you still are playing well for the game as it is at that moment. (This is really another issue. Many players who otherwise play reasonably well don't adjust their games enough when the game they are playing in becomes "super good." See *Getting The Best of It* by David Sklansky for more discussion on this subject.)

But too many bad players sitting at your table can have one very negative effect. Your swings (as measured by the standard deviation) will become bigger. In fact, they can become much bigger. This is easily seen by realizing that the pots will be very large and almost any card that hits may allow someone to draw out on you. Also, since the pots are so large, it now may become correct for you to "play bad." In my opinion, this makes these games tougher to play, and as I've already stated, many people who are otherwise successful players don't make the right adjustments for them.

Consequently, it appears to me that the best games would be those made up of about half good players and half terrible players. (Actually, the best games might be where half of your opponents are weak tight players and half are live ones.) Of course, exactly how well or how bad your opponents play can make a big difference, and exactly how their styles mesh with your style of playing also can impact your results. But I suspect that these "half-and-half" games are not only the most profitable, but also the easiest to play well.

Finally, I want to point out that just because a game has too many terrible players in it doesn't mean that it is bad. Obviously, just the opposite is true. You certainly can make money in a game where virtually everyone plays terrible. No-fold-em hold'em can be quite profitable, and two aces are not automatic losers, even though the large standard deviation that these games exhibit can at times make you doubt this statement. In other words, these games usually are neither as great nor as bad as some people think.

Technical Ideas
Afterthought

Technical ideas do play a significant role in poker, although they are only a small part of the overall game. What I have discovered, however, is that most players either downplay or neglect this area. I suspect the reason for this is that the typical player does not like to think or want to think "mathematically." (Actually, you should try to think "statistically," as opposed to thinking mathematically, but that is the subject for another text. See *Gambling Theory and Other Topics*.) That's too bad, because approaching poker in this manner would certainly improve most people's games, especially those who are just starting out.

One area that I want to touch on again is that of win rates and bankroll requirements. The typical person overestimates his win rate and underestimates his required bankroll. I believe this is the major reason why so many reasonably good poker players seem to always be looking for a stake. People tend to remember their good nights, when actually they were extremely lucky, and believe that these sessions are more representative of their play than they really are.

Another thing to keep in mind is that in general, the games get tougher as you move up. This is especially true at the larger stakes where many expert players can be found. Again, this means that the higher you play, the larger your bankroll needs to be, not only in terms of total cash, but in terms of "units" as well. This doesn't mean that you can't "take a shot," but *if your shot is not successful, you should quickly return to the lower limits.*

Part Three

Structure

Structure

Introduction

Structure is an area of poker about which much as been written in the past few years. Most people think that poker is poker. For example, if you can play hold'em, then you can play any type of hold'em, no matter how the particular game is structured. This isn't the case. How a game is structured — that is, the antes and/or blinds, the size of the bets, the number of betting rounds, and how the bet sizing changes from round to round — can be extremely important. In fact, it can turn some winners into losers and vice versa. More over, how a game is structured can mean that the particular game in question will thrive and grow or will quickly die out. As we will see, structure is a topic that should not be neglected. It is also a topic that at times can be quite controversial.

Limit Versus
No-Limit Hold'em — I

One of the things I've been told is that there is poker and there is no-limit poker. "The great players play no-limit." "It is a game of heart, mind, and courage." "You do more thinking in one hour of no-limit than in 24 hours of limit." "You are not a real poker player unless you play no-limit."

Is this really true? Should you be ashamed of yourself if you are just a limit player? Are you intellectually inferior if you don't push all of your chips into the pot at one time? Needless to say, I don't think so.

Taking a simple example from Texas hold'em, let's compare limit with no-limit play. Suppose in a multiway pot you flop top pair, it is a pair of jacks, and you are in an early position. How should you play this hand?

In *Hold'em Poker For Advanced Players*, which I co-wrote with David Sklansky, and which is written for limit play, we point out that this is a tough situation. Specifically, in today's modern structure, the bet on the flop in limit hold'em is often not large enough when compared to the size of the pot to make it correct for drawing hands — including holdings such as bottom pair — to throw their cards away. On the other hand, if you try for a check raise, hoping to reduce the field to a small number of players, and no one bets, the free card you have given may easily cost you the pot. In reality, the situation is usually much more complicated that what I have described. You also must consider the size of the pot, the texture of the flop, the number of players you are against, their playing characteristics, your kicker, whether the pot was raised preflop and its implications, and a whole lot more. Given these factors, doesn't seem like limit poker is an easy game; in fact, it is not an easy game to play at the expert level. No wonder some of the old-timers complain that in limit hold'em you cannot protect your hand.

Now suppose you are playing no-limit hold'em. The same situation would be quite easy. You would simply bet enough, perhaps about the size of the pot, to make it incorrect for a drawing hand to call. If someone does play, he is either making a mistake or you are in trouble. It is as simple as that, and bad players do make a lot of costly errors at no-limit hold'em.

This brings up another question: What has happened to the no-limit games? I don't know of any that are regularly spread in Las Vegas cardrooms or in the Los Angeles area, although some no-limit still gets played in the side action at a few major tournaments. I think the example just given demonstrates why these games have died out. No-limit was too easy to play well (at least many situations seem to me to be very straightforward) and if you didn't play well, you were quickly cleaned out.

Limit play of course is not like this. Although it's true that poor players will go broke in the long run, they can have some fun on the way. The edge that the expert no-limit player had on weak opponents was just too great, because often little doubt exists as to what the correct decision is, and when a weak opponent does not make the correct decision, he has only a slight chance and is usually severely punished for his error.

So why does no-limit still exist at the side games of major tournaments? Probably because some out-of-town suckers, who are fairly new to poker still think this is the game to play. However, there seems to be fewer no-limit (and pot-limit) games every year at the major events while limit games seem to grow larger and more numerous.

One world-class player has told me that if major tournaments had $10,000 limit final events instead of $10,000 no-limit events, "There would probably be many more entries." I agree.

Limit Versus
No Limit Hold'em — II

When the previous essay was first published, it stirred up quite a controversy. My claim that limit hold'em was more complicated than no-limit hold'em was more than some people could take. Of course, when I wrote this, I knew that the opinion I held was in the minority and that I would get some response, especially from other writers. I thought it might be interesting to continue this healthy debate and give my opinions on what two other writers had to say.

The first writer of interest responded that no-limit hold'em was much more complex than limit, "because you'll face many more decisions that matter." Well, I agree. You probably do face more decisions that matter in no-limit than in limit simply because you will look at or may want to make some very large bets. But that doesn't mean that no-limit is more complex. *In fact, this statement means nothing at all!* What one really needs to know to determine which game is more complex is *how difficult* is it to make the correct decision when it is a decision that matters. If it turns out that these decisions are all relatively easy to make in no-limit, then no-limit should be less complex than limit; if the opposite is true, then no-limit would, of course, be much more complicated.

Another writer, who plays mostly pot-limit Omaha (for very large stakes) and a lesser amount of no-limit hold'em, said that what I wrote was complete "rubbish." No problem with that. However, I found a later article by him to be quite interesting. He was giving some advice on playing "big-bet" poker. Specifically, he wrote the following:

> Fourth-street play is very important at both hold'em and Omaha. This is where scare cards freeze up the conservative players. All strong big-bet players have good "follow through." They are willing to back up the money expended on the flop with another barrel. A bet of the pot

on fourth street is likely to make an opponent release all but the best drawing hands.

Now I agree completely with these remarks, and I'm not even a no-limit player. The point is that they are *obviously* correct. But in limit hold'em, fourth-street strategies can be very tricky. In *Hold'em Poker For Advanced Players*, David Sklansky and I state that "you should probably check on fourth street as much as 60 percent of the time with your good and bad hands alike, as long as free cards are not a major problem and your opponents are aggressive." Notice that in this spot, unlike the no-limit example given by my writer friend it is not always clear what the correct decision is. That's just my point! It is not easy to figure out what the best limit strategy is, while in no-limit, it is much more obvious.

Another reason why limit hold'em is more complex is that you often go all in on an early round when playing no-limit. Any situation where you just look at the cards on fourth and fifth streets has to be much less difficult than when you are either faced with a bet or have the option to put your money in.

There is one other point that I want to clear up. The first writer also stated that "you'll have more fluctuations in the no-limit game, so pack your pockets with a bigger bankroll." Well, is this true? I don't think so. At least for the real experts, this should not be the case.

In *Gambling Theory and Other Topics*, I show that an individual's bankroll is predicated on two parameters. The first is your win rate, and the second is the standard deviation, which is the statistical measure of short-term luck (also known as fluctuations) that is present in a game. It is the relationship between these two parameters that determines one's bankroll requirements. *Even though it is true that the standard deviation is larger in no-limit hold'em, the real expert also will have a much larger win rate, meaning that he probably won't need as much money to ensure survival.* However, this is not true for the marginal player. The relationship between his win rate and the standard deviation will deteriorate, meaning that he will need a larger bankroll to play virtually risk free of going broke.

Another Problem
with No-Limit

As I've stated before, the no-limit structure gives expert players too much of an advantage over weak opponents, thus causing the games to die out. Another equally serious problem is that this structure makes the game too tight.

I'm not the first person to address the structure issue, especially as it concerns no-limit hold'em. Poker writer Bob Ciaffone has written about this topic many times and one of his chief complaints is that the structure of most no-limit hold'em games makes them too tight. World-class player Ray Zee also has pointed out to me that *the problem with no-limit hold'em is that the blinds are so small, you do not get punished for extremely tight play.* Of course, both men are right. In fact it is possible to be a consistent winner in no-limit hold'em and rarely play a hand, especially if you don't put much money on the table. Notice that in this situation, you will not get hurt much when you do play and lose a pot, but usually you still can be a winner when the night is over. Also notice that weaker players, who are always craving action, will become dissatisfied if they are in a game full of rocks.

(As an aside, this is one of the reasons I have argued that no-limit hold'em is not that difficult to play. On the other hand, if you do put a significant amount of money on the table and are willing to play a fair number of hands, then things quickly get much more complicated. By the way, if you play no-limit hold'em and are new to the game, it is probably best to follow this tight, little-money-on-the-table approach.)

So what is the cure for this problem? One possible solution would be to limit the amount of money that any player is allowed to put on the table. However, this would cause another set of problems that I don't want to get into because winning players would be required to go south with the money. It also would change the nature of no-limit hold'em. In addition notice that this would be the same as converting no-limit hold'em to a form of spread-limit hold'em.

Another possible remedy, which has been tried, is to make all the blinds the same size. At least this will sometimes automatically put several people in the pot. However, players who want to do so will now just play super tight on the flop.

So what's one to do? Well, one option is to play limit hold'em. In fact, many players are doing just that. Every year as I've pointed out, there seem to be fewer and fewer no-limit hold'em games but the limit games are stronger than ever.

Finally, I'd would like to emphasize that I am not also addressing pot-limit Omaha. In fact, I know less about this game than about any other form of poker. However, I am under the opinion that you cannot play pot-limit Omaha as tight as you can play no-limit hold'em and still be a winner, even though a tight approach is correct.

Why Limit Hold'em Is So Hard

In most forms of poker played in commercial cardrooms, there is a simple rule you can follow in almost every situation: *If you think you have the best hand, and there are more cards to come, bet!* Even though this rule is not perfect, it usually is not wrong by that much. For example, in the limit hold'em section of Doyle Brunson's monumental book *Super System*, Brunson states the following:

> One of the commonest methods for getting an extra bet is the check-raise. As you know, it's not a strategy that I use very much ... even in limit play.

Unfortunately, Brunson's remarks no longer apply to limit hold'em because the structure of the game has changed. When he was writing about it, $10-$20 hold'em had one and only one $5 blind. The bring-in before the flop was $5, the next player could either call the $5 or raise it to $10, and the bet on the flop was $10. Today's game has two blinds, the original $5 blind plus a $10 blind. Now the bring-in before the flop is $10 and all bets before the flop are in $10 increments, but the on-the-flop bet is still $10, just as before.

This change produces much larger pots on the flop, not only because the initial bet is bigger, but also because the double-blind structure encourages more multi-way action. This, in turn, has significant implications for correct strategy, and as a result, the rule previously given does not always hold anymore. In fact, the rule should now state: *If you have the best hand, stop and think about what you should do.*

Let's look at some examples. First, because of the large implied odds often available, hands that have long-shot potential — such as suited connectors and small pairs — have gone up in value mainly at the expense of unsuited high cards. Now this doesn't mean that a hand like:

is automatically playable. Indiscriminate play of this type of hand can be very expensive. But the idea that the initial before-the-flop bet is too large to make these hands profitable is wrong. When these hands can be played for profit depends on many things, including your position, your opponents, how well and how aggressive they play, how other players perceive you, and whether the pot has been raised.

Second, because of the modern structure, the bet on the flop is often so small when compared with the size of the pot that it becomes correct in many situations for your opponent to call with very weak hands. (Put another way, the bet is frequently not large enough to protect your hand.)

Suppose, for example, you have flopped top pair — perhaps a pair of jacks — you are first to act, and you have four opponents. Under the old structure, the correct play was to bet. But what about in today's game? Depending on the action before the flop, and on the number of other players who call your bet, a late-position opponent could easily be getting something like 10-to-1 on his call. If that's the case, what hands should he call with? Well, he is probably correct to call with just overcards (given that you have exactly a pair of jacks), with an inside straight draw, or with something like bottom pair, especially if he has a big kicker. If the pot is large enough, he may even be correct to call with one overcard that also has back-door flush potential.

It appears that the correct play in this situation is to check-raise. But if you try for a check-raise, and no one bets, the free card that you give could easily cost you the pot. And costing yourself a large pot, even if it is only occasionally, can easily be the difference between winning and losing.

In virtually all other forms of poker I am familiar with, this type of situation is not that common. In other words, if you like your hand, it is usually correct to bet.

Actually, the situation I have described is much more complicated than what this short essay indicates. Manipulating the size of the pot is an elaborate subject that does appear in almost all forms of poker, but it seems to make its presence felt more often in limit hold'em.

To further illustrate these points, I want to give an example of a hand I played in a $20-$40 hold'em game that was part of the side-game action at a major 1989 tournament. I held

and managed to get trapped in a large multiway pot that went to three bets before the flop. The flop came:

Notice that I had bottom pair and back-door flush potential. Also, if an ace hit, I may have had the best two pair. There was a bet and several callers before the action got to me. Since I was getting pot odds of approximately 25-to-1 and did not know for sure whether the person behind me would raise, I went ahead and called. (Also notice that even though my pot odds were 25-to-1, if I could get lucky, my implied odds were much higher.) Well, I did get lucky. I caught two running clubs and won a huge pot.

If the aggressor in an early position had just checked his hand then put in a raise, I never would have won the pot. However, even though he probably bet a good hand, his bet was not large enough to make my seemingly weak call incorrect.

So what's the conclusion? It's this: As I have been arguing in these pages, *limit hold'em is a very tough game to play well.* In fact, in my opinion, it may be the hardest of all common forms of poker to master. This doesn't mean that you can't become a great limit hold'em player, but to do so, you must acquire an enormous amount of knowledge and skill.

Spread Limit, Anyone?

If you are on a small bankroll, there is no question that the best game you can play, assuming that you play poker reasonably well, is spread limit. This is because you can achieve a higher win rate with significantly smaller fluctuations. Let's see why by comparing $2-$10 spread-limit hold'em with $5-$10 structured-limit hold'em. Suppose you are in a game that contains a live one who will always draw to an inside straight on the flop. Even though his play is usually incorrect, in structured limit the pots are sometimes large enough when compared to the size of the bet $5 that not throwing his hand away would occasionally be correct. In any case, making this play over and over again will produce only a moderate drain on his bankroll.

Now compare this to the spread-limit game. Not only are the initial pots almost always smaller, but also the bet on the flop can and should be about automatically double the size of the bet in a structured-limit game. Now when our live one makes his call, he is making a very big mistake. Specifically, the small pot that he can win every now and then comes nowhere close to making up for the large investment that is required. Consequently, our hero will quickly go broke, meaning that the expert player can win more than in a structured-limit game (with the same high bet). And since the fluctuations are also less, he needs a much smaller bankroll to survive.

One of the claims I've seen written about spread-limit games is that they require much more skill than structured-limit games because you have the option to bet different amounts on every betting round. Nothing could be further from the truth. While you do have the option to change your bet size, you basically want to see the flop for as little as possible if you have a drawing hand, but if you have a hand of immediate value, you want to charge your opponents as much as possible for the privilege of playing their drawing hands. (This may mean that you should call in an early position and then reraise if someone else raises.)

Once the flop comes, if you like your hand, you should just about always bet the maximum and give bad players the opportunity to make the biggest mistake possible. Check-raising is a strategy that should only rarely be used simply because the size of the bet is now large enough to protect your hand. Compare this to structured limit where the decision to either bet right out or to check-raise can be very complex because you often cannot bet enough to protect your hand. Consequently, you may be forced to try for a check-raise and risk a dreaded free card, which could easily beat you.

Another interesting thing about spread-limit games is that most cardroom managers realize how quickly bad players can get cleaned out, and therefore they resist spreading them. Notice the similarity to pot-limit and no-limit games, except that the stakes are much smaller. Cardrooms have learned that games like $2-$10 hold'em quickly wipe out the playing bankrolls of their tourists and weaker regulars, while in a game like $5-$10 hold'em, these same poor players can survive much longer and even have a few good wins. Again, remember that the bad player will still go broke in the long run, no matter what game he plays. But also remember that the cardroom will make much more money over the long run from structured limit than from spread limit simply because you can't drop anything if your game has burned out.

One final note: If you are a limit player, don't worry if you can't play spread limit. If you play well, there is still plenty of money to be made in the standard games.

Luck Versus Skill

One of the things I have stressed in my writings is that the best poker games are those where a good balance exists between skill and luck. If the game is too luck-oriented — that is, if it seems like the best hand just about never holds up, and it does not matter very much what cards you start with — then this game will not last or become very popular. (I believe this to be the problem with limit Omaha and is why "the game of the future" is only rarely spread anymore.) In addition, no matter how well you understand the game, you can't have a "real" win rate of any significance, but you certainly will have lots of big swings.

The opposite is also true. If the skill factor in a game is too high, meaning that poor players virtually never win, then it too will die out. This is the problem in no-limit (and pot-limit) hold'em. Bad players just stand no chance against the experts. Surprisingly, this problem also exists in some limit games. Let's talk about them.

The first game is spread-limit hold'em, particularly $2-$10 and similarly structured games where the pots are not big enough to punish someone for playing extremely tight. Also, errors in this game — such as draws to an inside straight — are very costly for the bad player since when he does hit his hand, the compensation he gets does not come close to making up for all the times he has missed.

Another game with an overly high skill factor is $10-$20 seven-card stud. Many readers might find this surprising since stud players often talk about the "roller coaster ride" they seem to be on. While this is true at $15-$30 stud and higher, the ante and bring-in at the $10-$20 level is just not large enough, compared to the bet to compensate for the type of errors that bad players make.

For example, suppose you hold a big pair, such as a pair of queens, and are called for a full $10 bet on third street by someone holding a pair of fours with a nine kicker. This call is certainly not a good play at a higher limit, but it is not nearly as bad as it is at

98

$10-$20. The bad player who is constantly making these plays at a bigger limit will slowly go broke; at $10-$20 he will lose his money at a much faster (relative) rate.

But there is another side to this story. If you can get in games where the antes or blinds are not large enough, and you have live players, you probably are in the best possible poker situation. In other words if you play reasonably well, you not only should have a high win rate, but your risk should be small as well.

Speaking of a high win rate, if you are game selective, you can easily win more in the long run in one of these games than you can at seemingly bigger games. For example, the better players at $2-$10 spread-limit hold'em can make much more money than the better players at $5-$10 structured-limit hold'em, and they need smaller bankrolls to ensure survival. This means that if games exist where the antes or blinds are too small, and if these games are not completely full of "rocks," many of you should consider playing exclusively in them. This is especially true if your bankroll is not too large.

Well, do any of these games exist? At present they do. In Las Vegas, no cardrooms are spreading $2-$10 but $2-$5-$10 spread-limit hold'em has appeared.[4] In the later game, all bets and raises on the first two rounds can be from $2 to $5, while all bets and raises on the last two rounds can be from $2 to $10. It's not quite the moneymaker as the $2-$10 structure described earlier, but is still a highly profitable game. Also, $10-$20 stud is hanging in there, but one of the rooms where it is currently spread has gone back to the old structure of a first raise to $7 on third street, which is probably a wise move for keeping the game alive in the long run.

---

[4]As far as I know, this structure was last spread in 1992.

Will Structure Ruin a Game?

Most readers believe that the smaller the ante, the tighter you should play. In general, this is true. However, it is the structure of *all* betting rounds, not only the initial ante size, that really should dictate whether and how a hand is played. To prove my point, we will examine two forms of seven-card stud: the $10-$20 game where everyone antes $1, the bring-in is $2, and the first raise makes the bet a total of $10, and the $15-$30 game where everyone antes $2, the bring-in is $5, and the first raise makes the bet a total of $15.

The conventional wisdom is that you should play the $10-$20 game tighter since the pot begins with 1.0 bets while the $15-$30 game begins with 1.4 bets. Usually this is correct. Let's look at a couple of examples.

For a steal of the antes and bring-in to be correct in the $15-$30 game, it must to be successful about 30 percent of the time. This includes those times when you are called but get lucky and win the pot anyway. (An example would be when you pair your upcard, forcing your opponent to fold. Also, if it were impossible for you to get lucky and win if someone else called, then a 42 percent success rate would be the correct number.)

Obviously, for a steal to be correct in the $10-$20 game, it needs to be successful more often since there is less money in the pot. This simply means that you should steal less in this game for the same number of players still to act behind you. (This assumes that everything else remains equal. If, for instance, your opponents are much less likely to defend in the $10-$20, game then it might become correct to steal a lot more often.) Consequently, the $10-$20 structure requires tighter play if you are thinking about raising on third street or calling someone else's raise.

Now let's look at another type of bet. Suppose the pot has not been raised on third street and you hold a marginal hand. You have the option of entering the pot for either $2 in the $10-$20 game or

$5 in the $15-$30 game. Notice that in the $10-$20, game you are hoping to get lucky and win future bets that are either 5 or 10 times the size of your $2 call. In the bigger game, if you get lucky, you will win bets that are only three or six times as large as your call. As a result these hands should be played more liberally in the $10-$20 structure.

What we are seeing is that the $10-$20 game currently has a structure where you should play looser in some situations but tighter in others. It wasn't always this way. In the past, the first raise in the $10-$20 game brought the bet to a total of $7. This meant that the stealing requirements were about the same as they were at the $15-$30 level (even though you were still inclined to play looser if you could just play for the bring-in). Consequently, the $10-$20 game was "balanced" more in line with the $15-$30 game, and it played similarly.

This brings me to the purpose for writing this essay. I understand that the main reason for changing the $10-$20 structure was to speed up play. Now the dealer doesn't have to make change as often since there are no longer any $7 bets. However, we are left with a game that encourages extremely tight play in some spots and extremely loose play in other spots, depending on whether the pot is raised on third street. The best poker games are not like this. Perhaps that is why there are many more $15-$30 seven-card stud games spread in Las Vegas than the $10-$20 variety. I suspect that poor structure is ruining this game.

Structure

Afterthought

As can be seen structure is a fairly controversial topic. It is also a crucial aspect of poker for those of us who play seriously, because games that are structured correctly will allow us to do reasonably well in the long run. If a game is structured too loose, the swings will be extremely great, and our real win rates won't be very high. If the games are structured too tight, we will do great while the games exist and live ones are sitting down. But eventually the games will die out and the bad players will find something else to play.

Before the legalization of stud and hold'em in California, players had a choice between two games, high draw or lowball draw. Almost all players would begin their poker careers by playing high. But once many of them discovered lowball — especially if they didn't play very well — they virtually never played high again. The reason was that bad players only rarely won at high draw. Lowball was, of course, a different manner. Although it's true that a bad player would still lose all his money at lowball, it took him a lot longer and he could have some fun along the way. Again, there is a lesson to be learned here.

Part Four

Strategic Ideas

Strategic Ideas

Introduction

Now we come to that area of poker where most of the money is won or lost. (This is especially true at the middle limits.) It is what I call "strategic ideas," and as we shall see, it covers a wide range of concepts and skills.

To me, implementing strategic ideas is simply the process of outplaying your opponents. It might mean playing tighter than certain other players in certain situations. It might mean anticipating what your opponent will do — that is, either check, bet, raise, or perhaps fold if you bet or raise. It might mean selecting the best game or the best seat in a game. It might mean manipulating your opponents in such a way that they make certain mistakes against you. For example, they may fold too often, allowing you to steal pots. Or it might mean blocking similar attempts to manipulate you into making mistakes.

In fact, strategic ideas can include many things. What follows only scratches the surface. But it is this type of thinking that separates the winners from the losers, especially as the limits get bigger.

Thinking Fast

What is it that separates great players from marginal winners? Is it a large amount of poker knowledge? Is it some magic formula on how to play the game that only a small group of successful players are aware of? Or is it just that these players are simply lucky like many people (usually those who lose their money to these experts) claim? If none of the above is true, then why do the same group of extremely successful players seem to win all the money year in and year out? And why is it that other extremely knowledgeable players always seem to run bad?

Of course, to be a great poker player, you do need to be extremely knowledgeable, and this knowledge does not come easy. Someone starting out can gain the requisite knowledge by reading and studying the few good books that are available. (See *Gambling Theory and Other Topics* for evaluations of many poker books and of other books about gambling. Also see the appendixes in this book.) In addition, a lot of thinking about the game — plus a great deal of experience — is absolutely necessary.

But there are many poker players who are fairly knowledgeable. They have done the necessary preparation, and even though they are winners at the game — and in many cases even support themselves playing poker — they are still nowhere close to being great players.

I have a friend who in many ways is one of the most successful players in the world. He does most of his play in the Los Angeles Clubs and plays regularly in the biggest games offered, often against some of the world champions. He has told me that players who normally play at the $30-$60 level are constantly taking shots at the $100-$200 and $200-$400 games, that these players just about never achieve a win over any reasonable length of time.

Why is this? Is it because experts at the $30-$60 level are not as knowledgeable as experts at the $200-$400 level? I don't believe this is the case. In fact, I doubt if there is much difference in what any of these players know or understand about the game. Without going into exactly how I came to this conclusion, I think that the real reason why some players always outperform everyone else has to do with speed of thought.

As readers of my material know, poker is a very complex game. (This is especially true if you play games like Texas hold'em or seven-card stud.) Moreover, you have only a very small period of time in which to make your decisions. This is normally not a problem since most decisions in poker are fairly straightforward. However, several times a night, if not more, you will be faced with situations that require a great deal of time to analyze, and you will not have that much time. It seems obvious to me that those who are able to quickly think through all the possibilities will have a significant edge over those who think at more normal speeds. (If you play extremely tight, you will have less of these troublesome situations to face, but you won't win nearly as much as the players who are able to successfully handle, through quick thinking, those times when they have put themselves in jeopardy.)

But this really isn't the whole story. You also need to think logically and to make sure that you take all the time you need to come to a proper conclusion. In addition, you must ensure that your ability to think as fast as possible is not impaired. This means that you should be well rested, should eat properly, should not drink and play, and of course, should stay away from drugs.

There is also a way to speed up your thinking process at the poker table. In fact, it has already been mentioned. It is simply to spend a great deal of time away from the poker table thinking about hands you have recently played, especially those hands that were major confrontations. Now, when you do get into a difficult situation that normally would require a lot of time to think through, you may have already considered something similar and might know exactly what to do.

Hold'em Poker For Advanced Players — A Few Comments

It has now been several years since David Sklansky and I released *Hold'em Poker For Advanced Players.* One question that often arises is exactly how good is this book? Here's my response. If you are a break-even $10-$20 player, if you study our text a great deal, and if you are well-disciplined (that is, if you don't have a major tilt problem), then in six to eight months you could be winning at a rate of $20 per hour, providing you do what the book says and your competition is not too tough. In another year, after you have accumulated a great deal of experience, your win rate should be even higher, and if you are game selective, it can be higher still.

However, the purpose of this essay is not to promote our book, but to warn those of you who do study the text of a couple of traps that are easy to fall into.

First, the book may encourage some players to play too loose. This is because a lot of the hands that we say to play are only playable in certain situations. And these situations — even though they do occur often enough to make them worth mentioning — occur only a minority of the time that you hold one of these hands.

I suspect that many of you who read the book will tend to forget the special conditions under which it becomes correct to play these hands. One of the examples we give is to sometimes call on the button with a hand like:

However, as we point out, calling with this hand is usually very costly.

Another example that we give in *Hold'em Poker For Advanced Players* is to sometimes play a hand like

in an early position. After we state why this hand can be played once in a while, we caution "Make sure that your hand is suited and only do it occasionally."

The second trap that readers of our book can fall into is to begin check-raising too much. One of the concepts we stress is that in today's modern structure, which very often creates large (multi-way) pots on the flop compared to the size of the bet, check-raising is an absolutely essential part of winning play. But this doesn't mean that check-raising is automatically correct every time you flop a good hand. Of course, the factors that you should consider are well-discussed in the text. They include things like who you are against, the effect of a possible free card, the action before the flop, how many people are in the hand, the texture of the board, and a whole lot more.

Here's an example. Suppose you flop a pair of jacks and it is top pair. Whether to check-raise with this hand can be a very tricky decision. Yet in some situations, risking the dreaded free card is easily the correct play. Notice that I said "some situations," not "all situations."

Even though I am warning against check-raising too much, most other writers on the game recommend that you hardly check-raise at all. Ironically, it turns out that we are both correct. The reason for this is that previous major works on hold'em (and there are only a couple) that discuss play after the flop were addressing a game structured much differently from the game played today.

Specifically, the bet on the flop was relatively much larger with respect to the pot size than it is in today's game. Consequently, in the old structure, check-raising as much as we recommend in *Hold'em Poker For Advanced Players* would not be an optimal strategy.

One thing to remember when playing hold'em is that playing tight, assuming that you play well when you do enter the pot, will get the money. While it's true that great players can play *a few more hands* than most people, they did not learn the skills that allow them to do this overnight.

Now You See It,
Now You Don't

Sometimes poker players are so tricky that the only people they trick are themselves. Here is an example of such a play that I observed one day in a $15-$30 hold'em game at the Stardust Hotel and Casino in Las Vegas.

The play began as follows. Before the flop, there was a raiser and a bunch of callers, and then the player on the button reraised. In all, there were six participants for three bets each. The flop came:

Everyone checked to the button, who bet, and there were three callers.

On the turn, another jack hit, and the first person, who held a pair of eights, bet out. (For those who don't know, the bet on fourth street in this game is twice the size of the bets on the previous rounds.) The next person folded, but the player before the button raised, forcing the button to fold. It appeared that the initial bettor was now also ready to fold, but before he could throw his hand away, his opponent showed him a seven.

This made things very interesting. The person showing the seven was a fairly tight player, and it would be improbable that he would call a raise with something like jack-seven suited. But after several people had already come in, it would be likely for this person to play a hand like a pair of sevens, hoping to flop a set (which he now had for certain). Since he liked his hand, he obviously was trying to lure a call.

What is interesting about this strategy is that the pair of sevens, who now held a full house, was making a terrible play. If the seven had not been shown, the raiser's most likely hand would be three jacks, meaning that there were only two outs left in the deck for the player holding the pair of eights. Since the pot was offering only 14-to-1 to call, a fold would be the correct play.

(In *Hold 'em Poker For Advanced Players*, David Sklansky and I talk about making these kinds of bets against typical players so that you can save money. If your opponent's raise does convince you that you are now drawing dead or close to dead, the correct play is to throw your hand away. However, notice that I said typical players. Against experts or sometimes "wild" players, a fold could be a significant error.)

But now the situation was different. Even though the raiser held a full house, which is certainly a better hand than three jacks, the pair of eights now had four outs instead of two. Consequently he needed approximately only 9-1 (if you include the implied odds of the additional action on the river) to make his call correct. (Another interesting thing concerning this hand is that three jacks is actually a better holding than the full house. This is an example of how hold'em sometimes plays very strangely.) Hence, by showing the seven and attracting the call, the holder of the full house made a significant mistake.

The outcome, of course, was devastating for the pair of sevens. (If it hadn't been I probably wouldn't be writing this essay.) A third jack hit on the river, giving the pot to the early position bettor who held the pair of eights. In addition, since it was correct for the pair of eights to call, this drawout should not be termed a "bad beat."

There is an important lesson to be learned from this example: In almost all forms of poker, unless you are absolutely sure that the trick play you are making is correct, it is usually best to win the big pots right away. Save your trick plays for the small pots. Then if your judgment is wrong and the play backfires, the penalty is not so great.

Weak Tight Opponents

In *Hold'em Poker For Advanced Players*, David Sklansky and I talk about a certain class of opponent that we refer to as "weak tight." The purpose of this essay is to clarify what we mean when we say "weak tight" and to discuss why this is in many ways the best type of opponent to play against. (Just to set the record straight, the first time I ever heard the term "weak tight" was in a discussion I had with world-class player Ray Zee.)

A weak tight player exhibits four characteristics: (1) he clearly will play fairly tight, (2) he usually plays in very predictable patterns, (3) he has the ability to fold marginal hands, and (4) he bluffs very little. Let's discuss these four characteristics in more detail.

Obviously, *anyone* who plays fairly tight is limiting the number of hands that he is likely to have. But the experts, even those who play very tight, have enough mix in their play to throw other players off. For example, in hold'em, the expert may usually call before the flop with a hand like

and raise before the flop with a hand like

112

But he also will reverse this strategy often enough that you can never be sure exactly where to "station" him. The weak tight player will play the same hands the tight expert will play, but he will not have a proper mix and will not throw off his better-playing opponents. This takes care of the first two characteristics.

Next, weak tight players can and will fold marginal hands. In fact, they seem so aware of the idea that bad players chase too much that they often look for excuses to fold their hands. For example, suppose in a hold'em game that you flop a flush draw, bet, and are called or perhaps even raised. Now the next card gives you a pair, but not top pair. Against a weak tight player, who is capable of laying down a lot of hands, your best play may be to try for a check-raise. Notice that if called, you still have a bunch of outs. However, against a loose player or an expert player, you should be less inclined to make this play, because it is profitable only when your opponent will fold some probable amount of time. If he will never fold, you have usually cost yourself money.

Finally, one of the reasons to play tight is that it makes your bluffs more effective. The weak tight player does not take advantage of this. In fact, when he bets or checks, he is giving away too much information.

Here's an example from high draw poker, jacks or better to open. Suppose your opponent, who has opened, draws one and bets. If he is a weak tight player, you should fold, unless you have a fairly strong hand yourself. But against an expert, who occasionally will open with a weak pair such as jacks or queens, even in early position, and will now draw one card and bet, you don't have an easy decision. You know that you are probably beat, but the pot may be large enough that you can justify a call. Of course, this is a position that you do not want to be in.

One last comment. Although weak tight players are great opponents because you can win lots of chips from them, I believe this type of play is the first step toward winning. In fact, most weak tight players will be small winners as long as they stay in small- to moderate-size games, usually $10-$20 and below. This is because even with their deficiencies, they still are playing much better than the tourists and many of their other opponents. However, at higher limits where many more experts can be found, weak tight players usually don't stand a chance.

To Bet or Not to Bet

To be a winning poker player requires several things: a very complete knowledge of the game you are playing, a good idea of how your opponents play, an understanding of how your opponents perceive you, and the ability to combine these things into a correct strategy. (Incidentally, when I say complete knowledge of the game, I am thinking in both mathematical and psychological terms.)

Following is a play I recently made in a $20-$40 hold'em game. As I will show, a different opinion of my opponent would have completely changed my action. By the way, this play is not that spectacular; in fact, it is rather routine. But it represents the type of thinking that separates the winners from the losers.

I had just sat down in the game and had posted a late-position blind of $20. A player in early position limped in, a middle-position player raised, and I called with the:

Then the player in early position who had just called, reraised. The other opponent and I now called.

Digressing for a moment, I had played with the reraiser many times before and was absolutely sure that he had either a pair of aces or a pair of kings. Even though other players would sometimes limp with ace-king suited or with just any ace-king, I thought this player would never do so. As I will shortly show, if my judgment had been wrong, the play I made on the end should have been different.

What happened was that I made the nut flush on fourth street and got to raise the original limper, who then called. (The other

115

player had dropped out.) However, there was also a king of spades on the board. On the river, the board paired fives, and my opponent checked to me. Now what is my correct play?

Clearly it is to also check. Since there are three kings and three aces unaccounted for, it becomes equally likely that my opponent has either a pair of kings or a pair of aces in his hand. This means that it is equally likely that he has a full house or an overpair, assuming that he would not throw the overpair away on fourth street when I raised. Notice that if he does hold a full house, I will be check raised, and if he has only the aces, I may not even get a call.

But suppose my judgment was wrong and this player also would have limped with an ace-king suited. Since I have an ace of hearts in my hand and the king of spades is on the board, this leaves only two possible combinations of ace-king suited. Now my opponent will have a full house three times, to an overpair three times, to a top pair twice. Even though I will have the best hand five out of eight times, because of the possible check-raise, it is still probably incorrect to bet.

Finally, suppose my opponent also will limp with any ace-king, suited or not. Now there are three ways I could be facing a full house, three ways I could be against an overpair, and nine ways I could be facing top pair. This means that I will have the best hand 12 out of 15 times. Clearly, even though I may be check-raised, a bet is correct.

Needless to say, when I did check on the end, I got some surprised looks when my hand beat a pair of aces. However, even though the above analysis is fairly straight-forward, couldn't I bet and then fold if I am check-raised? It turns out that the answer is yes and no.

Against weak-playing opponents, I could bet and fold if I was raised, because I would be absolutely sure that I was not being bluffed. But my opponent was not a weak player. I could not throw my hand away and be absolutely sure that my fold was correct (especially in a large pot which this one had become).

Consequently, I believed my best play was to check and hope that I had the winning hand.

One final note. Even though I said that these calculations were straightforward, I don't know of anyone who can quickly do them at the table. This is why it is important to spend some of your free time thinking about poker away from the poker table. Then when a situation like this comes up, you may immediately know exactly what to do.

Do Big Pots
Mean Good Games?

I walked into a cardroom recently and one of the people on the floor took me aside. "Mason," he said, "there is a great game going on that you should get into. Just look at the size of the pots!" Well, sure enough, the pots were huge, but that didn't mean it was a great game, or a good game, or even an OK game for that matter. In fact, I have become convinced that the best games, at least at limit poker, are those that usually have medium-sized pots. The games with huge pots are sometimes extremely lousy to play, even though many people think just the opposite.

There are basically three reasons for this. The first has to do with why the pots are so huge. Usually a couple of players are doing a lot of raising and reraising. Consequently, any hand you play will generally be very expensive especially on the first round of play. This means that the high implied odds many hands require to be profitable will not be available, simply because your initial investment will be so large. It also means that you need to be more selective about your starting hands, which implies that you won't have as many opportunities to outplay your opponents on the later rounds.

The second reason why these games are not the best deals with the possible mistakes your opponents will be making. The fewer mistakes your opponents make, the less your expected earn. One thing that happens if the pots are very large is that seemingly bad plays become correct. In hold'em, for example it becomes correct to draw to inside straights, not only on the flop but on the turn as well, if the pot is large enough. The same is true for hands like bottom pair and even for back-door flushes. In high draw, jacks or better to open, in double ante situations where the limit did not progress, opening with a pair of jacks, even in an early position, was usually correct. If you are against players who always make these plays, you want the pot to be small so that they are not correctly rewarded when the long shot does comes in.

The third reason why games with medium-size pots are best has to do with your opponents themselves. Players who constantly raise and reraise also usually do a great deal of bluffing (and semi-bluffing). And while their bluffing frequency may be too high for optimal play, especially if the pot is large, you still will not be sure where they are. In other words, you won't always know what you should do, and this can cause you to also make mistakes, especially if you are against more sophisticated players who are capable of changing gears. Just when you think they are bluffing too much, they may quit bluffing for a while, and the game becomes very tough to beat.

Contrast this to a game populated by "weak tight" players. Now, even though the pots are much smaller, which means that a higher bluffing frequency becomes correct, there is usually much less bluffing than in the game just described. (This is based on game theory ideas, which I will not go into here.) This means that you should have a better idea of what kind of hand you are up against and thus can play your hand more correctly.

By the way, if the pots are very small, indicating that the game is tight, this usually means a small earn for even the best players, particularly if your opponents also play well. Consequently, these games also should usually be avoided. An exception to this would be high-limit, seven-card stud where the high ante structure can make extremely tight games quite profitable if you can get away with a lot of stealing. Unfortunately, games like this are not very common.

Marginal Hands?

One bit of advice that I see every now and then is to play your marginal hands. The idea is that playing these hands is good for your image. That is, it is nice and to your benefit if your opponents don't think you are a rock or, worse yet, a "seat plug." In addition, you will be rewarded with lots of action later in the game if you are considered "one of the boys."

Actually, I agree with this. In fact, as long as you do hold a marginal hand, I think it is obviously correct to play it. The exception would be if you are on a small bankroll and are trying to reduce your fluctuations. As long as you know you have a hand that is either a small winner or a small loser in the long run, but you don't know which, then it seems only to your benefit to get into the pot especially if your opponents are perceptive. After all, over a lifetime of poker, these marginal hands won't cost you anything, and the game won't be nearly as boring. Moreover, it is a lot easier to be dealt a marginal hand than a good one.

However, I also see two problems with this. First, many of your opponents will not be very perceptive. Needless to say, these are the weaker players from whom most of the money comes anyway. Trying to impress the majority of them with how much action you give won't do a bit of good. So why take the risk, especially if there is some chance that the hand is not as marginal as you think. Also, if you have been "running bad," it is easy for lots of hands to look marginal, and for marginal hands to look good.

This brings me to the second problem. Notice that I said it would be correct to play hands that are either small winners or small losers. *But I wonder if these hands even exist. What I see are lots of hands that are either small winners or big losers in the long run.* An obvious example is a hand like in a raised pot in hold'em when you are neither in the big blind against a possible steal raise. While there are situations where it is clearly correct to play this hand, they seem to me to be few and far between. Perhaps I'm wrong, but I really believe that in many of these spots, *this hand, like most of the other so-called marginal hands, is either a small winner or a big loser.*

This brings me to another point. A hand that might be a big loser for an average player may actually be a small winner for an expert player. This is especially true in hold'em where the expert can give his weak-playing opponent a small head start and then outplay him on the flop and beyond. Consequently, the better players can play a few more hands in this game than the marginal players and win a little extra. However, in a game like limit lowball draw, even the experts do not have this luxury. In other words, just because you see a very good player play some questionable holding doesn't mean that you should do it. Moreover, even these experts cannot play too many additional hands.

Finally, notice that if you don't play your so-called marginal hands, you will be playing fairly tight. In fact, I'm convinced that it is hard to play too tight in many forms of poker. This has a lot to do with the structure of the games, which I won't discuss in this space. Of course, as I have just pointed out, the best players often can make these marginal holdings into small winners, and thus do successfully play them. Most of us, however, probably should leave them alone.

How to Become
a Great Player

I am an advocate of playing tight but aggressive. In fact, most so-called authorities also advocate tight but aggressive play. The reason for this is that it is correct. If for some reason you don't believe me, start playing loose and see how long your chips will last. In most cases, they won't last very long.

When I refer to a tight player, I also mean someone who plays fairly well. But there is a problem with playing like this. Even though you will be a consistent winner in the long run and can even make a nice living from the game, you won't become a great player. This is because tight players, who also play well, manage to stay out of those difficult situations that most of us would like to avoid when we sit down at the poker table.

On the other hand, if you play loose, you will get experience in situations where you are in great jeopardy. In fact, you may feel like you are in constant jeopardy (because you probably are). But one skill that all great players have is the ability to make the correct play most of the time when just figuring out the correct play is not an easy task. Let's look at a couple of examples.

Suppose you are a hold'em player. If you play moderately tight, one bad event that will rarely come up is flopping a set when someone else has flopped a higher set. If you play a fair amount, this will happen to you perhaps once every six months. But suppose you play loose. Specifically, let's assume that you always will call a raised pot before the flop with a small or medium pair, no matter what the opener's position is, no matter how tight he plays, and no matter how many players are in. Now you might make a few sets and get to look at some bigger ones. However, you also might become skilled enough to identify those situations where you are likely to be against a bigger set versus those times when you are against an overpair and have manipulated your opponent into giving you excessive action. Needless to say, the tight player will never get the experience necessary to develop this skill.

Next, let's suppose you are an ace-to-five lowball player. Some of the toughest hands to play well are the rough pat hands. This is because you are susceptible to bluffs, and good players will be able to extract the maximum amount of profit from you, even though the rough pat hand may actually be the better hand (heads-up) a majority of the time. The tight player just won't get himself into these situations. But the loose player, if he is to survive, will have to learn to tell difference between when he is being bluffed and when he is facing a real hand. Obviously, this is difficult to do, but some lowball experts do seem to be significantly better at recognizing bluffs than most everyone else. This might be because they have faced these situations more than their fair share.

Again, let me repeat my advice that tight but aggressive play is correct, especially for the vast majority of players. This means not only to be selective in what hands you play but also to make sure that you don't go too far with them when they are clearly losers. On the other hand, if your goal is to become great, playing loose will more likely get you there, assuming you don't go broke in the attempt.

Finally, in my conversations with several friends who also happen to be world-class players, their advice to me is to just about always play tight. But I wonder how many of them always listened to their own advice during their extremely successful poker careers.

The Best Hold'em Seat

Conventional wisdom has it that when playing poker you want the tight, passive players on your left and the loose, aggressive, and expert players on your right. This way you can trap the loose players for extra bets and stay out of the way of the aggressive and expert players, and those opponents sitting behind you won't extract the maximum from you when they are in position to do so. In general, I agree with this. I even give a statistical argument in *Gambling Theory and Other Topics* that supports this wisdom. It is very strong advice, and choosing the optimal seat at most games you sit in can make a significant difference in your win rate. But I'm not sure if this advice applies to hold'em, particularly in a structured-limit game such as $10-$20 or $15-$30 where there is a small blind and a big blind. Let's see why.

One of the nicest things that can happen to you when playing limit hold'em is to get a free play in your blind. In other words your opponents have only called, meaning that you do not have to put any additional money in the pot to play your hand. My guess is that in a $10-$20 game, if everyone passes to the player on the button and he now only calls, allowing you to play for free (in the big blind), this is roughly equivalent to him handing you $5 out of his pocket.

In *Hold'em Poker For Advanced Players* David Sklansky and I recommend that if you are in a late position and have a playable hand, to always raise if you are the first one in. This gives you the added equity of sometimes being able to pick up the blinds. The only time when this strategy might not be correct is against players who defend their blinds virtually every time.

So what does this mean if you are thinking about selecting a seat? Well, it obviously means that you want the non-aggressive players on your right, not on your left. It also means that you want the aggressive players on your left, not on your right where they are supposed to go according to conventional strategy.

If this were all there is to determining the best seat, we would be done, but unfortunately it is not. Once the flop comes and you have a whole hand to look at, things revert to normal. But even then there are exceptions. Sometimes you will get a flop that (if you understand the game) you will realize probably did not hit anyone. In other words, you may be in one of those situations where the first person to get his money in the pot wins. An example would be a flop like

where there was no raise on the first two cards. Here again, you probably want those aggressive players to your left.

In fact, even though this is an extreme example, flops that don't hit anyone, especially if not too many players are in the hand, do occur fairly often in this game. In these situations, being able to get your money in first, either on the flop or perhaps on a later street if no one bets the flop is very profitable.

But this doesn't mean that you want an expert on your left. He may realize that it is doubtful you have anything and will try to make a play to take the pot away from you. As you can see, this is one of those situations where the correct answer is hard to figure.

So what's the bottom line? It's this: When playing hold'em, try to consider more than the usual factors when selecting your seat. Also consider how well *each* of your opponents plays and how you think he will react to your game. The best seat may be as far away as possible from the expert. By maintaining some distance you will minimize your confrontations with him.

Selecting the Best Game

The poker games in Las Vegas and elsewhere can be very tough. When I say "tough," I mean that virtually all of your opponents will play at least reasonably well, and your win rate in the game, assuming that you also play at least reasonably well, will be small at best. In fact, you might not even be able to beat the rake or collection.

There are essentially two situations where the games become very tough. The first is at very high stakes where the contest is being played shorthanded among a few experts. This situation actually makes sense. What these pros are doing is waiting (hoping) for a live one to sit down. At very large stakes, these experts can make a pretty decent living, even if they get to play against a sucker only every now and then.

The other situation isn't so logical. It occurs at the middle limits, and the table is usually full. The stakes are generally large enough to guarantee a pretty good expectation if the game is good, but I have seen line-ups where I did not think that anyone had much of a win. Why does this occur?

I believe the answer has to do with the players' egos. If you sit in one of these games, and most of us have at one time or another, and ask the expert next to you about the expert sitting across the table from you, you almost always will be told that "he can't play." What's interesting is that the expert across the table from you will tell you the same thing about the expert sitting next to you. No wonder some games are so terrible. In fact, many experts would have a higher "earn" if they played in a smaller game than the one they usually play in.

Changing the subject slightly, once you reach a certain level of competence at poker, your most important decision by far is game selection. It is well worth the time spent looking at games in different cardrooms until you find one that you like. At the very

126

least, you should examine the different games offered in the same cardroom.

So how do you tell if a game is any good? If you are a regular player, one obvious way is to try to find a game where you don't know most of your prospective opponents. I only rarely find an unknown player who, as it turns out, actually plays well.

Another way is to watch a game and see how tight and aggressive the players are. The ideal game is where everyone just calls. Keep in mind that big pots do not necessarily mean that the game is good. In fact, if the big pots are being caused by a lot of raising and reraising, the game may not be good at all.

A related idea is to be ready for good games that you expect to occur. For instance, the side action at the major poker tournaments can be quite profitable, even if you are only an OK player. This means that when the tournament comes, you should be ready to play. Don't stay up all night just before the side action is ready to start and be too tired to play when the games get really good. Also, just because the table is full of "live ones" when you sit down doesn't mean that it will stay that way. If a game has gone bad, and they very often do, make sure that you are able to leave, or to at least change games, even if you are stuck.

One final concept is to try to become proficient at more than one type of poker. Sometimes in Las Vegas the hold'em games aren't very good, but the stud games can be great. The opposite is also true.

A World-Class Play

I thought I would give an example of a world-class play that I recently observed in a $30-$60 razz (seven-card lowball) game. The reason I want to discuss this play is that it is the type of play that wins the money, especially in the bigger games where to be successful you must be able to really play "poker." The play occurred between an extremely strong player who we will call Player A, and a fairly tight opponent, who we will call Player B. (By the way, the reason I used razz in this example is that of all forms of poker, it is one of the simplest. Even so the reader will see that this play was quite sophisticated.)

Here's what happened. Player A opened the pot for $30 with the following terrific hand:

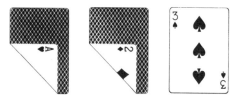

He was called by Player B, who had the 7♣ up, and everyone else folded. On fourth street, Player B caught the 8♥ while Player A caught the J♦. Player B bet and Player A called. What's unusual about the play is that against most opponents, Player A would have thrown his hand away. (He had caught a bad card compared to his opponent's good one, and the pot was not that big.) But against B, who plays well, he called. Why would he do this?

The answer is simple. Because Player B plays reasonably well by most people's standards, Player A now has two ways to win the pot. First, he might outdraw his opponent, and second, if he catches the right scare cards (namely an ace or a deuce) and Player B catches bad, he might be able to steal the pot because B will think he is probably drawing dead. Notice that against most people, this second way of winning the pot does not exist since they will call you down anyway, no matter how hopeless the situation may appear.

The hand was played out as follows. On fifth street Player A caught the 2♥ (which paired one of his hole cards but still looked scary to Player B), and B caught the Q♠. Player A bet and B called. On sixth street A caught the 8♣ and B caught bad again. Player A bet and B threw his four-card eight-seven away, convinced that he was drawing dead. If Player B could have seen A's hole cards, he would have kept playing. In fact, he would have been quite irritated that he quickly threw his hand away, even though against most opponents this was the correct decision to make.

Again, the reason that this play was so good is that Player A would make it against only a very small number of opponents. If Player B was also world-class, he might have been able to figure out that a possible play had been put on him. He should realize that since the pot was not that big, A would call on fourth street only if he had a terrific starting hand, probably a three-card wheel. This means that any extremely small card should now be suspect, especially if B understands that Player A is capable of playing for this type of steal. Obviously Player B did not grasp these ideas and allowed Player A to manipulate him out of the pot.

This is an example of how the best players are able to win much more than tight players. They do this by simply out thinking them. Tight players never understand this and usually complain about how lucky certain big winners are.

Changing the subject slightly, I have a friend who is easily one of the best players around. Whenever I ask him how he would play a particular hand, his answer invariably begins with two questions: "How well do you play compared to your opponent, and how well does your opponent think you play?" The point is that in many situations, there is no one "correct" way to play a particular holding. How a hand should be played and what strategies you should use in the later rounds is sometimes more dependent on your abilities, the abilities of your opponent, and what you think your opponent's perception of you is than on the cards that are on the table.

Sometimes when the combinations are right, you can make plays that most tight players would never even consider making. These types of plays come under the heading of "counter strategies." (Those of you who want to read more about counter strategies should see *Sklansky on Poker*.) They require a great deal of thinking both at and away from the poker table and can add significantly to your profits when correctly executed. They also can be quite costly when your judgment is not as accurate as it needs to be. However, counter strategies are absolutely necessary to be successful at the higher limits (that is, $30-$60 and above).

Common Seven-Card Stud Errors

At the time of this writing, I don't play as much stud as I do hold'em, but I do play enough to see certain errors commonly made by many regular players who play the middle-limit games. Following are a few of these common mistakes.

(By the way, there is much more to seven-card stud than what is covered here. Four good sources of information are Doyle Brunson's *Super System*, Mike Caro's *Professional Seven-Card Stud Report*, *Seven Card Stud For Advanced Players* (written by David Sklansky, myself, and Ray Zee), and David Sklansky's *The Theory of Poker*.)

Error No. 1: Playing dead hands. This is probably the most common error made by typical seven-card stud players. Having a hand that has the maximum potential to improve is most important. This doesn't mean that you should throw away something like a pair of aces on third street just because one of your aces is out. But how live your hand is can greatly impact its value. Some hands that normally are playable should hit the muck even if they are only semi-dead, while other holdings that are completely live can sometimes be played, even though most players will always throw them away.

Error No. 2: Trying for a flush with many suited cards out. This idea is, of course, an extension of the one just given, but let's examine it in detail. Suppose you are in an eight-handed game, which means that you have knowledge of 10 cards — the eight upcards, plus your other two cards. Table I gives the probability of completing your flush and the odds against completing your flush, assuming that you started with three suited cards and based on the number of additional suited cards that are exposed.

Table I: Probability of completing a flush

Other Exposed Suited Cards	Prob	Odds to 1	Other Exposed Suited Cards	Prob	Odds to 1
0	.2345	3.3	4	.0910	10.0
1	.1957	4.1	5	.0629	14.9
2	.1579	5.3	6	.0391	24.6
3	.1229	7.1	7	.0202	48.5

In reality, a rational person would not make a flush this often since he frequently would throw away hands that still had the potential to back into a flush. Notice that the difference between zero other exposed suited cards (3.3-to-1) and three exposed suited cards (7.1-to-1) is highly significant. (I would be willing to bet that many readers are surprised at how great this difference really is.) This means that if more than two other suited cards are exposed, the hand is probably not worth playing unless it has some other sort of value, such as high cards or straight potential. Similar reasoning applies to straight draws.

Error No. 3: Entering a multi-player pot with a pair of face cards when your hand is not very live. This is another example of the same idea. Suppose you enter a pot with a pair and a fairly worthless card. Table II gives the probability of improving to different hands, assuming you stay for all seven cards. (By the way, these probabilities will change slightly, depending on exactly what your pair and kicker are.)

Table II: Probability of improving when you hold
a pair and a worthless card

Hand	Prob	Cum Prob
Straight Flush	.0000	.0000
Four of a Kind	.0054	.0054
Full House	.0757	.0811
Flush	.0070	.0881
Straight	.0085	.0966
Trips	.0989	.1955
Two Pair	.4205	.6160
One Pair	.3840	1.0000

Now suppose that one of your rank is exposed. Table III gives the probability of improving to different hands, assuming that you stay for all seven cards. (Again, these probabilities will change slightly, depending on exactly what your pair and kicker are. In addition, the probabilities in this table were estimated using Mike Caro's *Poker Probe*. The probabilities in the other two tables were computed directly.)

Table III: One of your rank is exposed

Hand	Prob	Cum Prob
Straight Flush	.0000	.0000
Four of a Kind	.0003	.0003
Full House	.0534	.0537
Flush	.0076	.0613
Straight	.0077	.0690
Trips	.0533	.1223
Two Pair	.4567	.5790
One Pair	.4210	1.0000

Notice that if one of your rank is exposed, you will make a set or better a little more than half as often as you will if none of your rank is exposed. If other cards that would help your hand are also dead, the situation will be even worse. The conclusion is that in a multi-handed pot where two pair often will be beat, having a hand that is not live is usually enough to make it unplayable.

Error No. 4: Calling the bring-in and then feeling committed to playing the hand. Let's look at an example. Suppose you call the bring-in with something like:

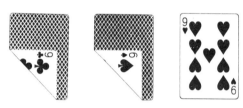

Then there is a raise and a reraise behind you. It is now almost a certainty that there is a much better hand out, especially if both the raiser and reraiser have higher exposed cards than your own. You will pay a large fee for the privilege of continuing to play and you will be in a situation where even if you improve to two pair, your hand can easily be beat. It's true that in stud you often want to chase a large pot when the pot odds make it worth doing or when your hand has much more potential. But in the situation just described, it is best to fold. The small call invested should now be written off as a small loss. Continuing to play and risking a probable large loss is simply not worth it.

Error No. 5: Just calling with high cards when you are first in. One of the reasons to play a hand like three high cards is to be able to pick up a small pot. It is very hard to steal these pots unless you raise. Only calling the bring-in may mean that you eventually get beat by a weak hand. In addition, playing high cards against several active players is usually a big mistake. At best you have a marginal hand, and at worse you not only are chasing but may be against quality draws as well. Remember, in seven-card stud it is difficult to get out of a pot once you have an investment in it. With hands containing only high cards, you want to end the action quickly. Calling won't be the solution; either raise or pass.

Error No. 6: Immediately throwing away your hand when you have the smallest card up. Occasionally, I see a player throw his cards away at the same time that he throws the bring-in into the pot. He obviously not only has a small card up but two other terrible cards as well. Usually, when a player does this, he is just showing the frustration of running bad. The problem with just throwing a hand away is that you never know what will happen at a poker table, simply because *one* of the ingredients that make up a poker game is probability. Put another way, you never know when you will get lucky. It is possible that no one will raise (forcing you out), you might get a free card on fourth street, and you might be in a powerful position by fifth street. Always give your opponents the opportunity to make mistakes against you. In addition, showing frustration helps make you a target — in some player's minds — which can easily work against you in the future.

Error No. 7: Failing to reraise when your exposed pair is higher than the high card of the raiser. Suppose the pot is raised by someone with a queen showing, and you have a pair of kings with a king up. The correct play is to almost always reraise. There are three reasons for this. First, you probably will reduce the competition to just the two of you; second, you may trap another player between the two of you for additional money; and third, if someone else does call for the two bets, he may be making an expensive mistake. In addition, just calling does not completely disguise your hand. To call his raise, your opponent knows you probably have something, so a possible pair of kings should be one of his suspicions anyway. Also, in case the player with the queen up does not really have a strong hand, if you don't win the pot right there with the reraise, your opponent may be hooked into calling you all the way to the end.

Error No. 8: Trying to steal when someone has already called the bring-in. It is almost always a mistake to try and steal once someone has voluntarily entered the pot, even if he has only called. There are many reasons for this. First, many players who have committed to a pot in seven-card stud find it very difficult to fold, even when folding is obviously the best decision. Second, a few players will often attempt to play their hands deceptively on third street; that is, when these opponents come in, there is a reasonable chance that they are stronger than their call indicates. Third, seven-card stud, because of the seven cards, is a great draw-out game, and raises on the early streets just won't drive some players out. Fourth, the smaller bet size on third street, when compared to the bet size on the later streets, will also keep many people in. And fifth, many players who just call the bring-in with small pairs and small kickers incorrectly believe that these hands can stand a raise.

Error No. 9: Calling an early or middle-position raiser when his exposed card is higher than your medium (or small) pair and your kicker is small. Suppose you have

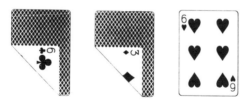

and someone with a queen up raises from an early position. Is it correct to call? The answer is that unless you know this opponent extremely well, it is almost always best to drop. The reason for this is that your opponent is less likely to steal when up front. Consequently, it is improbable that he will represent a hand he does not have. Now this doesn't mean that he has to have two queens. For example, he may have raised on a high three-flush. But it is very likely that he does have some sort of hand. As a result, the probability is high that you will be chasing from the beginning, and at this stage in a seven-card stud hand, you are not getting the proper odds to chase.

Error No. 10: Regularly playing high exposed pairs deceptively from an early position. Suppose you are in an early seat, have a high exposed pair, and decide to just call for the purpose of letting other players in. There are several things wrong with this play. First, because of your position, your opponents will know that you hold something and will be suspicious of your hand anyway. Second, some of your opponents who now will get in cheap may have played anyway for a larger bet. Thus you may have cost yourself money in the long run. And third, remember that it is probably easier in stud than in any other high poker game to draw out on your opponents. Consequently, if you give other players good odds to draw out on you, it may actually become correct for them to attempt to do so, and this will cost you money.

By the way, there are times when it is correct to limp in up front with a big pair. These occasions are discussed in *Seven-Card Stud For Advanced Players*.

Error No. 11: Playing medium and small pairs deceptively. This error is usually seen when a late-position player, who is the first one to voluntarily enter the pot, just calls. The consequences are the same as those for playing high exposed pairs deceptively. However, this mistake not only increases the chances of being beaten but is compounded by the fact that the holder of the pair is sacrificing his chance to pick up the antes. This is especially true in a game with a large ante structure where it becomes difficult to win — unless the game is very loose — without stealing the antes every now and then.

Note: Even though the most important decision that one makes in seven-card stud occurs on the first three cards — to play or not to play — this doesn't mean that the other streets can be neglected. The thrust of what follows is to recognize those hands that either are no longer playable for profit or can be played for profit as long as the correct strategy is followed. Even though it is often correct to chase in stud, the idea of continuing to play because the pot is large in relation to the size of the bet is not always correct, simply because one's implied odds can be very negative. In other words, one's hand, when compared to other holdings, loses too much ground on each successive card, and the skilled player can extract too much money from it.

Error No. 12: Calling when your opponent pairs his door card. You don't need to play seven-card stud very long before you realize that when your opponent pairs his door card, it is extremely dangerous. Even so, it is just very difficult for most players (me included) to get away from some hands. Now there are times when it is correct to keep playing when your opponent pairs his door card, but in general, you should throw your hand away. This is especially true on fourth or fifth street before the pot has gotten too big.

Error No. 13: Neglecting to check-raise. Since it often makes sense to chase in stud, it also makes sense to try to limit your opposition when you hold a reasonably strong hand. An excellent way to do this is to check-raise. You want to check-raise when the last person to act is a very aggressive player, and it is likely that everyone else will check to him. This strategy may even be correct if you probably have the second-best hand, but you think it is close. By the way, don't overuse the check-raise. If you do, some of your more observant opponents correctly may begin to fear your checks more than your bets.

Error No. 14: Not passing on the later streets if betting has been light. Often on fifth street, and especially on sixth street, it is correct to chase. This is because the pot is usually so much larger than the bet size that the probability of drawing out on your opponent(s) makes chasing the correct play. However, you must consider the pot size. It is not necessary to chase if the betting has been light on previous rounds. Of course, this situation is most likely to occur on fifth street. Also, light betting is in relation to the current bet size. Remember, the pot odds are approximately cut in half on fifth street in the bigger games where the betting limits double.

Error No. 15: Not betting into probable come hands on the later streets. Suppose you are very sure that an opponent has four cards to a flush, and you have no reason to believe that he has anything to go along with his draw. If this is the case, make your opponent pay for the privilege of drawing out on you. In fact, your bet will minimize the profit he makes on his drawing hands, simply because flush and straight draws with one or two cards to come are (usually) missed more times than they are made.

Error No. 16: Failing to bet medium-strength hands. Pots tend to get very large in seven-card stud, meaning that it is correct to call with weak hands. Consequently, when holding a medium-strength hand, it is usually profitable to bet on the later betting rounds. The best thing that can happen is that the weak hands will fold, giving up the chase. The time not to bet is when you are absolutely sure that an opponent holds a much better hand, and he is likely to raise. However, if you don't think he will raise but will bet if you check, it may be better to bet. (This is especially true if there are available scare cards may make your opponent fold on a future round.)

Error No. 17: Failing to raise with a second-best hand. Since the pots get so large in seven-card stud, being able to improve your chances of winning the pot — even if you improve them only a small amount — becomes very important. This means that it is often correct to raise with a second-best hand to knock other players out, even if you are fairly sure that the bettor currently has you beat. The idea is to raise with a hand that has a fairly good chance of becoming the best hand if you can play heads up against the initial bettor. Even though you might be reraised, it is still often worth this gamble.

Error No. 18: Failing to bet scare cards. One important play in seven-card stud is to bet your hand if you think the card you have just caught might allow you to win the pot on the next round should you catch another threatening card, and if there are a lot of scare cards left in the deck for you to catch. This play is especially important on fourth street since the bet on the next round usually doubles.

Note: Finally, we come to seventh-street errors. Even though many players think there is no strategy to be employed on seventh street, correct winning play is actually quite creative. In other words seventh street does not play automatically.

Error No. 19: Not calling. Without a doubt, losing a big pot that you should have won is a terrible poker error. By the time the last card is dealt, the pots are so big in seven-card stud that to throw your hand away, you need to be absolutely sure that the bettor has you beat. Of course, if this is the case, you should release, but this means that you have to know your opponent extremely well. In other words, even though that final call is usually a losing effort, it is almost always correct to make it.

Error No. 20: Failing to bluff on the end. Even though it is correct to do a lot of calling on the end in seven-card stud, this does not mean that everyone does it. Moreover, there are some bluffing opportunities at the river that are not routine ones. They usually occur when your opponent's board and the play of his hand indicate that he obviously has only a medium-strength holding. Your bet will convince many players that they must be beat. However, do not make this bluff against someone who can't lay down a hand.

Error No. 21: Checking blind on the end when you have an obvious flush draw. The main reason some people check blind on the end is to stop an opponent from either bluffing or value betting. But these are precisely the types of bets that you want someone to make when you are on a draw. This means that if you are going to check on the end, which is often a mistake anyway, you should always look at your cards and let your check show that you are "truly weak."

Error No. 22: Failing to bet aces into a dead board. Suppose you are against an aggressive opponent who has a weak board showing. If you check two aces and this player has made two pair, he will usually bet, and because of the size of the pot, you will almost always call. However, if you bet, again because of the size of the pot, you may get called by some hands that cannot beat a pair of aces. This means that even though a pair of aces may be a losing hand, they may actually lose less if you bet them than if you check. This is especially true if many of the cards that you think your opponent needs have already been put out of play. The exception to this would be if you are against an opponent who is likely to bluff.

Error No. 23: Failing to be aggressive when your opponent has represented your high hidden pair. Here is an example. Suppose you have a hidden pair of kings, and your opponent who has a king up (on third street) has represented a pair of kings by betting strongly from the beginning. If you make a hand like kings-up, and if it is clear that your opponent is not trying to complete a straight or a flush, be prepared to raise on the end. This is not only because that king is a dead card, but also because a likely hand for this opponent is a smaller two pair.

Final note: As stated in the introduction, this advice is not enough to make you into a winner. But these ideas if utilized might help you plug some holes in your game.

The Effect of a Maniac

A maniac is a player who not only plays too many hands but also constantly raises and reraises with them. Maniacs help create huge pots and most people think they are great for the games. In fact, many players go out of their way to try to get maniacs in their game. But is the maniac an ideal opponent? I don't think so.

In my experience, the best games are loose and passive; that is, you are against very little raising but always have lots of callers when you do make a hand. So what's wrong with having a maniac in your game, especially one who is known to lose a fair amount of money. Some concepts are discussed below.

Concept No. 1: The maniac will cause other players to tighten up. This is probably the most significant problem with having a maniac in your game. Most typical players, whether they are overall winners or losers tend to play too loose. But because of the way they react to a maniac, their games usually will become tighter and they will begin to play much better. This means that in general, the game will become much tougher. Even though the maniac may lose his money, you won't be the only one to get it. In fact, you may now be able to get only a small piece of it, if you get any at all. In addition, other players from whom you expect to win in the long run now may actually be winning from you. This would be especially true if you fail to adjust to the fact that they now may be playing substantially tighter.

Concept No. 2: The maniac should make you throw away hands that are dependent on high implied odds. Some starting hands that you play for profit at the poker table are really hands that have little value on the first round but that have potential to win a big pot every now and then. These are hands like three-flushes in seven-card stud and medium suited connectors in hold'em. But, if you can't get in cheaply, many of these holdings should be quickly thrown away. Obviously, the maniac makes a lot of these hands unprofitable. The high implied odds that these hands normally have (and need) will not be available because of the large initial investment that will now usually be required.

Concept No. 3: The maniac will cause you to "play bad." Even though the maniac may lose a lot of money, by making the pot very large, he makes it correct for the expert to "play badly." For instance, if enough bets are in the pot, drawing to an inside straight, even if it may not be the best hand if completed, becomes correct. This is the type of play that many bad players will automatically make. One reason why the expert makes money is that he plays differently from the typical player in many situations. The maniac has the ability to change this. That is, even the best players will at times correctly begin to "play badly."

Concept No. 4: The maniac often will force loose passive players to play better. In my opinion, one of the best opponents to be against is the loose passive player. This is an opponent who plays lots of hands but plays them predictably and non-aggressively. The maniac, by his constant raising, may deprive these loose players of being able to play many of their weaker hands that they automatically would be in the pot with otherwise. Even a sucker won't play a longshot holding if it costs him several bets. Notice that if this happens, there won't be any more weak loose players in the game. As pointed out in Concept No. 1 above, the maniac has now succeeded in making the game much tougher.

Concept No. 5: The maniac will sometimes cause you to lose control of the game. This is another major problem with a maniac. One thing that an expert player does is manipulate his opponent into making mistakes. This happens because weak players often will react predictably to certain bets and raises and when certain scare cards hit the board. Obviously, a maniac won't do this. In fact, the maniac may react just the opposite. (For example, he might play back with very little when you are trying to buy a free card or ignore your raise on the previous round and bet into you on the next round.) This is a situation that winning poker players would like to avoid.

Final Note: Again, I want to point out that maniacs are losing players. The point is that even though this is true, maniacs not only make the game more difficult to play in, but encourage some of your opponents to play much better as well.

Your Opponent Makes a Difference: Part I

Following is an example of an expert play at the hold'em table. This is the type of play that I see very few people make but that can be crucial to being successful at poker. It is also the type of play that separates the real experts from the everyday (tight) players.

Suppose that you are in the big blind and hold the following hand:

Further, suppose that there is a raise from a player in an early player, two players behind the raiser call, and you call. (Notice that your call is very marginal at best since you can easily flop a queen and be outkicked.)

Now the flop comes:

You bet since you do not want to give a free card to anyone even though you are not sure that you have the best hand. The player in early position (who was the original before-the-flop raiser) calls, and everyone else folds.

The fourth-street card is the:

What is your play? Notice that your options are to bet, to check with the intention of folding, to check with the intention of calling, and to check with the intention of raising. Also, if you bet and are raised, you may want to fold.

The answer in this spot is interesting since (like many other plays in poker) it depends on the skill of the player you are against and on what you think his perception of you is. Suppose your opponent plays very well. If that is the case it is unlikely that he would call on the flop with something like

since the players behind him could easily raise, and you could then reraise. In addition, he would not be that confident that he would win the pot if an overcard hit since a likely hand for you or for someone behind him is A-Q or K-Q. This means that it is more probable for your opponent to have a hand like

or an overpair. And since giving a cheap card is not that dangerous with this flop, he may be waiting to raise on fourth street. The correct play against this particular opponent is to try for a check-raise on fourth street (representing an eight), hoping your opponent will throw his hand away. However, if you believe your opponent may think you would try this type of play with a weak hand, then it may not be correct.

Against a weak player, your play is just the opposite. Now you want to bet on the turn. This way, if your opponent does have overcards (which is now more likely), you do not give him a free card, and if he does have an eight (which is also more likely), you can fold when he raises. This is especially true if he is the type of player who now would raise only with at least three eights. Also notice that since your opponent is a weak player, it is not likely that he will be able to throw away a good queen if you do check-raise. He will just decide that he has to pay you off since he will think his hand is pretty good.

The situation would be somewhat different if the fourth- street card had been the 8♣, giving you a flush draw, instead of the 8♦. Now you would still check-raise the good player for the reasons previously stated but it would probably be best to check and call against the weak player. The reason for the check and call is that it is not as likely that you are drawing dead when the weak player raises since another club can also win the pot for you.

As can be seen by this example alone, poker can be quite complicated. No play, especially in a game like Texas hold'em, is set in concrete. The correct way to play a hand not only depends on your hand, your position, and what you think your opponent may or may not have, but also on how well you think your opponent plays. (By the way, this can change from moment to moment. If your opponent is currently steaming, his play can be much different from what it normally is.) In fact, as the example shows, how well your opponent plays is sometimes the most important criteria of all.

Your Opponent Makes a Difference: Part II

When playing seven-card stud, which is better, a split pair of aces or a buried pair of aces. (For those who don't know, a split pair of aces is when one of your aces is your upcard, and a buried pair of aces is when both of your aces are in the hole.) This question came up in a game I was playing in not too long ago. Two players were discussing the issue and one of them argued that he preferred to have the aces split. In fact, he argued very strongly that having one of the aces up was best. Just about everyone will tell you that this person was wrong. After all, when the aces are buried, you have not only a strong hand but a great deal of deception as well. Is this true? Well it depends.

Let's look at an example. Suppose someone with a king up raises, and a weak player with a six up reraises. Furthermore, let's assume we know that if the weak player was rolled up, he would virtually never reraise, and we are not looking at a "maniac" who just might reraise with anything. (By the way, at the middle limits, many people do play just like this. They always wait until either fifth or sixth street to raise with their rolled up hands and only reraise on third street with big pairs that they think are most likely the best hand.) So what is the weak player's hand? Obviously, it is a pair of aces in the hole. Since you know not only what his pair is but what his kicker is as well, and you may want to keep playing. If the aces were split, you would not have so much knowledge about his hand, and it probably would be correct in most situations to throw away something like a pair of kings. This is because you can never be sure when he makes two pair. Put another way, knowing what someone's kicker is makes his hand much weaker. This is true even if his kicker appears to be a fairly harmless card.

Next, suppose a strong player reraises in the same situation. Now you can't be so sure about his hand. Other than having aces in the hole, he could be rolled up, have just a pair of sixes with an ace or a king kicker, have a very live three- flush with an ace in the hole, or perhaps have three straight-flush cards. It seems like this strong player is better off having the aces buried.

This brings up an interesting concept that very few poker players ever consider. It is: "How well do you play, how well does your opponent play, and how well does your opponent think you play?" What this concept means is that particular hands may change their values depending on who is playing them and on who that player is against.

Here's another example. It is obvious that two aces in hold'em is the best hand, no matter what the situation. But what about a hand like:

Well, this hand can dramatically change value depending not only on the situation, but also on how well both you and your opponent play.

For instance, if you find yourself (most likely) heads-up against a strong player who raises coming in, you should just about always throw your hand away. This is because you have too much catching up to do for the price you have to pay.

But what if you find yourself against a weak predictable opponent, especially someone who is quick to throw his hand away if he does not flop anything. Now you may occasionally want to play. In fact, some of the times you play, you may even want to reraise.

When making this reraise, you need to consider what your opponent thinks of you. If he believes you are capable (or even likely) to reraise with this type of hand, you should only rarely, if ever, do it. This is because it is now more likely that your opponent will be willing to pay you off with a relatively weak hand.

On the other hand, if he thinks you play really tight, this type of reraise occasionally may be very effective. (Even so, I would still do it only occasionally.) Notice that if no one flops anything, you will be likely to steal the pot. If an ace comes, as long as your opponent does not hold an ace, you may be able to steal even if your opponent has made something like middle pair.

An interesting thing about poker is that many situations that appear similar to someone who is not an expert player are actually quite different. This essay has given two examples but there are also many others.

Playing Short-Handed: Part I

I like to stay up all night and sleep most of the day. It's not a bad life, but if you are a poker player, there is one draw back: Many poker games break up, or at the least, some of the players leave. This means that I often find myself playing short-handed. Many people don't like to play under these conditions. I believe the reason for this is that very few players really understand how to play short-handed games. However, those who do grasp the differences between full and short handed games probably will do quite well.

By the way, I believe it is much more difficult to play well in short-handed games. This is because you have to do a great deal of thinking in pots that can be contested by only a few players and where certain hands do not play automatically. Let's get specific.

The most important difference between short-handed and full games is that the psychology of the game and players usually changes. Many plays and situations that appear to be mathematically or strategically similar actually play very differently. Let's look at an example.

Suppose you are sitting in a $10-$20 Texas hold'em game that requires one $5 blind and one $10 blind. You are on the button and hold

and everyone else has passed. What should you do in a full game?

The answer is easy. Usually raise and hope to steal the blinds. However, if you don't succeed in stealing the blinds, you might be able to steal on the flop or on a later street, or you might get lucky and flop a strong hand. Notice that you have two ways to win. One is based on stealing, and one is based on the relatively small chance that you do make something.

Now suppose you are in a three-handed game, are on the button, and hold the same hand. Also, notice that from both a mathematical and strategic point of view, the two situations appear to be similar. In fact, having this hand in the short-handed game might be even better. This is because when a lot of people pass in a full-handed game, it implies that high cards are left in the deck, meaning that players in the blinds are a little more likely to have strong starting hands. (By the way, this effect is not that strong in hold'em, but in a game like ace-to-five draw lowball it can be significant.)

However, even though this hand may be better to have in a three-handed game, I believe the correct play is usually to throw these cards away. Although you may want to call or even to raise occasionally, it's generally best to just muck your cards because the psychology of the game has changed. Your opponents expect you to raise, and they are psychologically prepared to mix it up. They don't expect you to be very selective in the hands you play since the blinds come around so quickly. This means that typical players are going to call or occasionally even reraise with a lot of hands that they would normally throw away in a full game. Consequently, stealing is much more difficult in this spot than it normally is. In addition, it also becomes harder to steal on the flop and on the later streets.

Put another way, the eight-seven suited doesn't have the value that it has in a full game. For example, in a two-handed pot, would you rather hold the above-mentioned hand, or would you prefer to be playing:

I'm not saying that a hand like king-rag is superior to a middle suited connector in a short handed game; that is a completely different subject that is too lengthy to discuss here. But do keep in mind that many hands change value when the game becomes short-handed. Pairs and unsuited high cards go up in value while hands like the middle suited connectors go down in value. Those players who do not make these basic adjustments will have no chance in short-handed games.

Playing Short-Handed: Part II

This essay discusses some specific concepts that should aid anyone playing in short-handed situations. However, if you have not played much short-handed, don't run out and find the biggest game available after you finish looking over these ideas. Successful short-handed play, like successful poker in general, requires a good deal of experience. Start small and slowly work your way up.

Concept No. 1: Understand that many hands change value. Here's an example from hold'em. Suppose you are on the button in a full game, everyone has passed to you, and your hand is:

What should you do? The answer is simple. As long as conditions are normal, you just about always should raise. When you do this, you have two ways to win. First, you may steal the blinds, and second, if someone calls (or reraises), you may get lucky on the flop and make a strong hand.

Now suppose you are in a three-handed game and are again on the button with the same hand. What is your play? If you raise, you probably will be called. This is because in a short-handed game, people expect you to raise, and they will not fear your raise as much. In addition, your opponents will be further encouraged to play since they have to take the blind so often.

Consequently, this hand should be thrown away in most cases. Notice that this middle connector has gone down in value and when this type of hand goes down in value, then hands like unsuited high

154

cards, small pairs, and just an ace or even a king with a weak kicker are now worth much more.

Concept No. 2: Try to play hands that can win by themselves. Since you will be called much more often, it is now important to play hands that can win by themselves in short-handed pots. An obvious example of this is playing any ace in hold'em. If no one hits the board, an ace often will win the pot.

Concept No. 3: Be prepared to go to the river. Notice that in short-handed games, you and your opponents will be attempting to steal the antes or blinds a lot. This means that when you call, unless the board develops in a very scary manner, you should be prepared to go all the way. In other words, you should now be more willing to play a showdown contest. Consequently, remember to stick with hands that might be able to win the pot without improving.

Concept No. 4: Don't be as afraid of scare cards. This is an extension of some of the ideas already mentioned. Specifically, since your opponent is much more likely to be on a steal, you should not be as afraid of threatening board cards as you would be in a full game. For example, when playing seven-card stud, if your opponent catches a suited high card on fourth street, you should not be as quick to fold your medium pair. This is because it is now more likely that a threatening board is all he has. As usual, when making these types of decisions, you must consider who you are against, how he perceives you, and so on. But in general, you should call a much higher percentage of the time when you have a couple of opponents than you would if the table was full.

Concept No. 5: Understand that tight players are less likely to play in short-handed games. One type of moderately successful player you run into a lot at the poker tables is someone who plays tight but not very creatively. Sometimes we refer to these people as "weak tight." In any case, this is not the type of player who usually wants to sit in a short-handed game.

The reason for this is simple: Weak tight players do not want to post a lot of blinds, and they don't want to be in a position where they are constantly calling raises. This means that in general, you need to adjust your strategy for a much faster and looser game.

Concept No. 6: Be willing to check and call more. Again, this has a lot to do with the opponent you are up against and how likely you think he is to bluff. However, remember that in short-handed games, it is much less likely that you will be against a tight player who is content to grind out an earn. In fact, you probably will be against a fast, aggressive player who is willing to try to run over you, especially if you are perceived as someone who plays very tight.

Hold'em —
Loose or Tight: Part I

Figuring out a correct hold'em strategy can be difficult. Specifically, should you play loose or tight? Many successful players play very tight, but there are other successful players who play a lot of hands. Which way is correct? Is playing tight always the best approach? Or does playing loose allow you to win more money?

These are tough questions to answer, and they are questions that most hold'em players wrestle with when they are trying to determine how they should play. The purpose of this essay and the one that follows is to examine the reasons for playing tight and those for playing loose. Let's start with the reasons for playing loose.

Reason No. 1: In hold'em there is a large element of luck on the flop. One of the unique things about hold'em is that your hand changes dramatically between the first two rounds of betting. Consequently, many hands that at first appear a lot weaker than some other hands can become very strong holdings after the flop.

Put another way, you don't really have a hand in this game until you see the flop. This means that the difference in value between many hands is not as great as it seems, especially if many players have entered the pot. As a result, hands that appear unplayable to someone who is not highly skilled at this game may actually be profitable if you have a pretty good idea of how your opponent plays.

Reason No. 2: You can outplay weak opponents on the flop. Many players do not fully understand how hands change value once the flop appears. This means that the expert often can outplay his weaker opponents after the flop, especially if the flop is favorable to his hand or very unfavorable to his opponent's likely hand. Consequently, if you play very well, you can give many of your opponents a small head start and still play profitably against them.

Reason No. 3: You can play more hands in late position. Of all forms of poker, hold'em is probably the most position-oriented. This is because the game's blind structure predetermines the order in which the players act on all four betting rounds. And since it is usually advantageous to act last in poker, you can play more hands in the late positions than you can in the early seats. This is particularly true if you are on the button or have a good indication that the players to act behind you will throw their hands away.

Reason No. 4: The blind accounts for part of the bet. The main reason for adding blinds to any form of poker is to stimulate the action. This is because many hands that may not be worth a full bet are easily worth a partial bet. So obviously, when playing hold'em, you can correctly call with many hands out of the blinds, especially from the big blind, that would be correct to throw away in many other positions.

Reason No. 5: Your opponents are passive. Having opponents who do not take full advantage of any edge they have over you is very important. Needless to say, this allows you to play many more marginal hands and to play them in an earlier position since you will not be punished to the degree you should be when someone else has the best of it. You also can consider playing more hands if your passive opponents remain passive on the flop and beyond. This is because the free cards you get occasionally allow you to win a pot that strong opponents would never allow you to win.

Reason No. 6: Your opponents are weak tight. One thing that happens in hold'em is that the flop often will not hit anyone, particularly if there are not many players in the pot. This means that against opponents who are quick to throw their hands away, you can bluff more in this game than in any other form of limit poker.

Consequently, you can play more hands against this type of opponent since you have the added equity of a successful bluff in many situations.

Final Comment: I am sure there are many other reasons to play loose in this game. But keep in mind that how well you play and how well your opponents play have a lot to do with whether a loose style of play is correct for you.

Hold'em —
Loose or Tight: Part II

In the previous essay, I gave a number of reasons for loose play in limit Texas hold'em. Let's face it, this is the way we would all like to play. It is certainly a lot more fun to play a lot of hands in any poker game than to just sit there watching. However, when playing hold'em, there are also reasons to be very selective with the hands you play. Let's discuss some of them.

Reason No. 1: Hold'em has a small blind structure. When I say small blind structure, I am referring to the fact that to see all hands that taking the blinds entitles you to see does not cost very much. Put another way, you do not get punished in this game for playing very tight. This means that if you decide to sit there and play only your very strong hands, it will not cost you very much even if this is not the correct strategy for the game you are in. This is especially true if you do not play well or do not have much experience in this game.

Reason No. 2: Your hand may have bad implied odds. When playing hold'em a hand like:

is sometimes a pretty good hand. But if there are already a lot of people in the pot, even if there is no raise and you are in a late position, it may not be profitable. This is because in multi-way pots hands like small pairs and the medium suited connectors go up in value because they have lots of people to collect from when they get lucky and make a strong hand.

Who do they collect from? They collect from exactly the type of hand described above — that is unsuited high cards. This means that it is sometimes correct to throw a hand like A♦T♣ away when you are in late position in an unraised pot even though it is often a raising hand in this spot. (For more discussion of this concept see *Hold'em Poker for Advanced Players*.)

Reason No. 3: You are in an early position. There are several things wrong with playing hands from an early position. First, there may be a lot of action behind you that either may force you to throw your hand away or at least might make it very expensive for you to continue playing. Second, since you must act before many of your opponents on all betting rounds, your check or bet will give them much information about the two cards you are holding. And third, if your kicker is not very good, you may run into the problem discussed in Reason No. 2.

This does not mean that you should throw away virtually every hand you are dealt in an early position. There are a lot of things to consider besides just your position. These include the cards you are holding, how well your opponents play, how well they think you play, and how aggressive the particular game is.

Reason No. 4: You may be against overpairs. Suppose you have a hand like

and you are against an opponent who has two larger cards. If this is the case, it certainly is correct to go ahead and play. However, there is a small chance that you will be against an overpair. If that is the situation, playing should be very expensive in the long run.

Although the chance of an overpair is slight, if you are against someone who plays tight, and if he raises, indicating a stronger than normal hand, it is very unlikely that he is on a possible steal. Consequently, unless many other players are already in the pot, this hand should be thrown away.

Reason No. 5: You may be against aggressive opponents. This is the same concept that was discussed in the previous essay, except now we are looking at the opposite situation. If you are against aggressive opponents who are willing to punish you in case you are holding a marginal hand, then you should be much more selective in deciding which hands to play. Also, try to consider what these players think of your play. If they do not have much respect for you, either because they don't think you play very well or simply because they don't think about these kinds of things, then again you should limit the number of hands that you are willing to play.

Final Comment: As can be seen by these two essays, whether to play loose or tight in hold'em is not an easy question to answer. A lot depends on how well you play, how well your opponents play, how they perceive you, etc. These things should sound familiar to most readers.

Front Loading, Anyone?

As most readers know, a great deal of money has been won by a small number of highly skilled blackjack players. How did they do it? Did they just learn one of the well-known card counting systems and then clean up, or was there some other method that was sometimes used?

Well, there is another technique, known as front loading, which is a method of looking at the dealer's hole card. It takes a lot of practice to master this skill, but I understand that this is the skill that took down the real money.

I won't go into how you front load in this short space. But if you are interested, there is a book I wrote titled *Blackjack Essays* that explains the correct technique.

However, there is a good reason for bringing up this topic, it is the fact that you occasionally can front load at the poker table. Sometimes a sloppy dealer pitches the cards too high, which means that if you are sitting in an appropriate seat, usually next to the dealer, you may be able to see some of your opponent's hole cards. As most readers will quickly realize, this is quite an advantage.

But how many poker players have this skill? Just to set the record straight, I don't. The information on front loading that appears in my blackjack book was supplied to me by some friends who are experts in this area.

There are, however, a few poker players who have developed this skill. I currently know of three people who have had some success with front loading at the poker table. But I think there are more front loaders sitting at the poker tables than most people suspect, especially since many highly skilled blackjack players have adopted poker as their new game.

In addition, there are a couple of well-known, world-class players who have an uncanny ability to pick off bluffs. Perhaps they have developed front-loading skills and sometimes know for sure that they are looking at a busted hand. However, I have no reason to believe that this is the case with any particular individual.

A point I want to make is that front loading definitely is not cheating. Although I feel it is somewhat unethical, this information is available to all players at the poker (or blackjack) table. Consequently, players who are able to front load are not doing anything wrong; it is the cardroom's responsibility to make sure that its dealers follow proper procedures.

However, I recommend that you speak out and "correct" any dealer you see pitching the cards too high. Even though it's unlikely that someone is getting an advantage on you, it is always possible that there is a front loader in your game.

By the way, dealers who spend a great deal of time talking and don't pay attention to the job they are performing — and there are a small number of these — become candidates for front loading. Also, break-in dealers who are new to their profession may be susceptible to front loading. This is another reason why only the better dealers should be allowed to deal the larger games.

Strategic Ideas

Afterthought

As can be seen, strategic ideas cover a wide range of topics, and this small number of essays probably only scratches the surface. However, one concept should shine through: *How well do you play, how well does your opponent play, and how well does he think you play?*

Notice that this concept came up over and over again in the essays. In fact, there are few poker situations where you should not consider it. For example, suppose you sit down in a poker game, and everyone at the table is a complete stranger to you. (This may occur when you are out of town or playing in the side action at a major tournament.) The first thing you should do is try to figure out who the good players are. Next, try to figure out what these good players think of your game. Once both these things are determined — assuming you play fairly well and can adjust correctly to your conclusions — you should be a significant money favorite in the game.

Obviously there is more to poker than just this one idea. Many of the essays in this section and in the rest of the book have already stressed that. But properly implementing this concept is an absolute must to winning play.

In addition, keep in mind that to be a successful poker player, especially at the higher limits, takes a great deal of skill and experience. Many things need to be considered when making your decisions. What is correct in one situation may be completely wrong in another, even though the two situations may appear very similar.

Also, don't get discouraged because you are struggling with your game. You may be having just a "run of bad luck." But if your bad luck continues over a fairly long period of time, it is likely that there are major deficiencies in your game. A friend of mine who plays well likes to say that it is good to run bad every now and then. As

165

he puts it, "Running bad makes me play better." The reason for this is that poor results make him think about his play and review many of the strategies he uses. This is something that we should all be doing. However you don't have to wait until you start losing to adopt this practice.

Part Five

Image

Image

Introduction

Image is an aspect of poker about which a great deal has been written. It is also an area of poker that I don't consider very important. It seems to me that if you play well, your image will take care of itself. Yet statements like the following one appear in the poker literature all the time: "The poker experts agree. A powerful table image is an important tool in winning play."

Well, I'm one of those so-called experts, and I certainly don't agree. Poker, as I have stressed many times before, is a very complex game. To be successful at poker, you must have a great understanding of the game and of the people you are playing against, as well as a great deal of experience. Besides this, you need to do a lot of thinking about what you are doing, and your thinking needs to be done in a logical and orderly fashion.

It seems to me that many people consider image as one of those "magic bullets" that will make things easier for them. But poker is too complex for this to be a winning formula. Image does play a role in winning play. But in my opinion, it is a small one, definitely not the dominating force that it has been made out to be.

Where Did My Image Go?

I see it in print all the time, and the players I know tell me constantly, "You must have an aggressive image." Let's face it, we all know that if you don't have that aggressive image, there is no way you can win playing poker. But if you play aggressively, and everyone knows this, you probably will never lose a pot. And if you do happen to lose one, then obviously you got unlucky, because there certainly can be nothing wrong with your play. Besides, all the top players play aggressively, so why shouldn't you.

Clearly, from the way I wrote the preceding paragraph, I don't agree with the idea of being constantly aggressive. In fact, there are many times at the poker table when the correct strategy is to play passively and see what happens. Sometimes you should do this when you most likely have the best hand, even though your hand is not strong enough to slow play.

Let me give an example of a hand I observed in a $20-$40 hold'em game that I was playing in at a major Las Vegas cardroom. In the game was one of those super-aggressive players (who, of course, can't understand why he has run so badly) who made an extremely terrible play.

The hand came down as follows. Seven players had only called the $20 blind until our super-aggressive player raised with

in the big blind. Of course, everyone called. The flop came ace high with no draws, and our super-aggressive player bet and was called in three spots. On the turn came a five, which seemed harmless enough, but it made a set of fives for one of the callers, who was in a late position. Needless to say, our super-aggressive player now proceeded to lose three double-size bets and also to inform the winner of the pot how stupid he was.

But was the winner of the pot so stupid? Because of the preflop raise made by our super-aggressive player, the player holding the pair of fives was getting pot odds of 19-to-1. In reality, if you consider the three double-size bets that the pair of fives probably would get if he did make his hand, his true (implied) pot odds are at least 25-to-1 and may be as high as 30-to-1, depending on what kind of action he actually does manage to get. Clearly the pair of fives was correct to call the bet on the flop. The person who played poorly was the super aggressive player who never should have raised with his ace-jack offsuit before the flop.

In *Hold'em Poker For Advanced Players*, David Sklansky and I write about a concept which until publication of that book, was probably understood by only a small number of extremely successful players. The concept is to manipulate the size of the pot so that your opponents most likely will play their hands wrong if you happen to get a flop to your liking. What this means is that sometimes you should raise with hands that don't seem to warrant it, such as with a small pair if many people are already in, and sometimes you should call with hands that most people think are clearly raising hands.

For example, ace-jack offsuit is clearly a preflop raising hand in many hold'em situations. But there are times — and many readers just won't believe this — when it actually may be correct to throw this hand away before the flop in an unraised pot and you are in a late position. (See *Hold'em Poker For Advanced Players* for more information.)

So what's the bottom line. It's this: *Poker plays should be made simply because they are the best plays.* Correct strategy should be based on solid mathematical, strategic, and psychological reasons. Plays should not be made because you are striving for some silly image. However, if strong play does produce an image that somehow intimidates your opponents into making terrible mistakes, then so much the better. Remember, if our super-aggressive player had not raised before the flop, then the pair of fives would have been making a mistake to call on the flop, and theoretically our super-aggressive player would have been making money. On the other hand, by raising before the flop with the ace-jack offsuit, he was theoretically losing money. These are the type of plays that contribute to being either a winner or a loser in the long run.

Appropriate Image

One aspect of successful poker play is what I like to call "appropriate image." The idea is to match your image to the game you are playing so that you can manipulate your opponents, allowing you to win more money. I don't consider image to be a major part of winning play since I believe that if you play strategically well, your image will take care of itself. However, following is what I think are the best images for five different games. By the way, I am only addressing middle-limit play, that is, games from the $10-$20 through the $30-$60 range.

Before we start, here is my criterion for appropriate image. Basically, you want to see what mistakes your opponents are making and then encourage them to exaggerate these mistakes. For instance, if your opponents are calling too much, you would like them to call every time. If they are not calling enough, you would like them to fold every time. Also, the following is what I believe to be generally true, but a particular opponent may behave much differently.

Game No. 1: High draw, jacks or better to open. The major error in this game is that a poor-playing opponent calls too much, especially if he holds the joker in his hand. This is true both before and after the draw. Since most pots are not too large, incorrect calls can be significant errors and add a great deal to your profits. Consequently, the best image is one of a loose lively player. Somehow, you should only rarely bluff but make your opponents think you bluff all the time. One way to accomplish this is to raise with marginal hands in certain positions where it is correct to do so. An example is to "pop" a late-position opener with a pair of aces and then to draw three.

Game No. 2: Ace-to-five lowball. Before the draw, most poor-playing opponents call too much, but after the draw, they don't call

172

nearly enough. The before-the-draw error is not too costly since the edge between many lowball hands is not that great. However, after the draw, those opponents who will not call when they are last to act with something like a jack or a queen are making a serious mistake. This implies that the best image is tight but aggressive. The ability to steal pots can easily turn an otherwise marginal player into a significant winner.

Game No. 3: Texas hold'em. One of the characteristics of hold'em is that you do not flop enough hands. Also, some flops appear where it is likely that none of the cards showing have hit anyone's hand. (An example would be 9-9-3 of three different suits.) This means that the ability to steal pots is crucial in this game. Consequently, a tight but aggressive image is most important, perhaps more important in hold'em than in any other game. The exception would be against very weak opponents (who are perhaps new to the game) who don't yet understand that calling with one overcard with several players still to act behind them can be suicide. In these games, you will just have to show your opponents a hand.

Game No. 4: Seven-card stud. Many players in this game do play too many hands on third street; on the other hand, the pots quickly get so big that it often becomes correct to chase. The exception is when your opponent's board has become very scary. Perhaps he has paired his door card or has something like a four-flush showing. Again, this means that the ability to steal a pot, even just every now and then, can add significantly to your earn. Since the pots do get extremely large, it is only rarely wrong for your opponent to call on the end with a weak hand. However, throwing away the winning hand in this game is clearly a disaster. Again, a tight but aggressive image seems to be what one should strive for.

Game No. 5: Razz. For those who don't know, razz is seven-card stud played for low. The major error that bad players make in this game is to call on an early street when they shouldn't. For example, assuming that you started with a good three-card hand and you catch a baby on fourth street, if your opponent has caught bad (either he now has a big card or he has made a pair), you would like for him to call. The best razz players seem to have the ability to gain these calls. They do this through non stop talking that at times can be irritating to their opponents. The conclusion is that in this game, as in high draw, a loose lively image is what one should strive for.

When Is a
Dynamic Image Good?

It seems that several poker writers are constantly pushing the concept of a dynamic image. The idea is that by behaving in a certain eccentric or perhaps forceful way, you can get many more calls. This, in turn can dramatically increase your profits. There was a time when I was very intrigued by this concept and supported it in some of my writings. But today I have a much different opinion. I believe that a dynamic image is very useful in certain simple forms of poker. But for many other games, it is just the opposite type of image that one would like to project. In fact, I believe that in most forms of poker widely played today, a dynamic image can be extremely expensive.

First, let me state that no form of poker is really very simple. But the fact is that some games, such as razz (seven-card stud played for low), are relatively easy when compared to other forms of poker, such as seven-card stud or Texas hold'em.

Let's look at an example from razz. Suppose on third street, you and your opponent each start with three good cards. But on fourth street, you catch a baby and your opponent catches bad. If you can get your opponent to call in this spot, you have gained a lot. In fact, this is one of the key places in the play of a razz hand where (theoretically) much money is either won or lost. But the problem is that almost everyone who plays the game — with the exception of the very worst players — knows that folding is the proper play. However, suppose your image was strong enough to get some people who know better to go ahead and call. Then your dynamic image would be making you a great deal of profit and would clearly be a major contributor to your profits.

One thing I've noticed is that some of the most successful razz players have this type of image although "dynamic" would not be the correct word to describe the effect their behavior has on their opponents. "Annoying" or "irritating" might be a much better term.

But in any case, the fact that they do get these calls definitely adds to their profits. Consequently, those individuals who exhibit this type of image — and who also have a good understanding of the game — should do quite well at razz.

Another relatively simple game where a dynamic image pays off is high draw, jacks or better to open. An example is when you are the opener and you can get someone to call you with a pair smaller than jacks (known as shorts). Again, this is a play that is obviously wrong to most participants, but bad players will make these plays, especially against someone whose behavior somehow entices them to stay in the pot.

One of the reasons why a dynamic image is successful in razz and high draw is that the pots tend not to be too big. In other words, an extra call here and there makes a significant difference.

But what about a game like seven-card stud? Now things are much different. One of the problems in stud is that because the pots get so big, it is often correct to chase. This means that a dynamic image ensures that many of your opponents will play correctly against you, especially on the later streets.

For example, one of the ways that you make money in seven-card stud is to occasionally steal the pot on the river. An opponent who incorrectly throws his hand away on the end can easily be costing himself seven to 10 big bets. In addition, if you are an expert player, and you do make this mistake, it could take you an expected five to 10 hours to recover the money you just lost.

So in conclusion, what's the image that you want in this game? I doubt if dynamic, wild, loose, or crazy would be correct. In fact, the most successful players I know are regarded by most of their opponents as being very conservative. Stud is not the game in which the crazy man gets all the money. One world-class player explained it to me this way. "Mason," he said, "when a top player calls you, you should feel a little sick."

Put another way, in seven-card stud, as in all forms of poker, to be a big winner, you need to play very well. And, as I like to say, *if you act like Bozo the clown, expect to do as well as Bozo the clown.*

It's How You Are Perceived

I wish to clarify a few things concerning my opinion on "image." It seems that any time I write on this topic, it has the potential of being greatly misunderstood and therefore, often creates a controversy.

First, although I do not believe image is very important, I agree that it does play a role in winning poker strategy. In fact, at the higher limits, how your opponents perceive you and your understanding of this can be crucial to winning play. What I think is silly is other writers constantly advocating a dynamic, loose, and wild image for complex games like Texas hold'em and seven-card stud. While this is the correct image to have in relatively simple games, such as high draw and razz, it is not the "magic formula" in other games and will be quite costly.

In fact, I cannot think of any top players, and I know many of them, who are perceived by their opponents in this fashion. Part of the reason for this is that in games like hold'em and stud, you make a great many more mediocre hands than you do the nuts. Put another way, you need to steal pots in these games if you want to be a winner. That's why semi-bluffing is so important, especially as you get into the bigger limits. If you don't understand this, you might as well just kiss your chips good-bye.

Let me give an example. Suppose you are playing hold'em, and your first two cards are:

You and three other opponents each put in two bets before the flop, and the flop comes:

Notice that there are now (including the blinds) about nine bets in the pot. Also notice that you are now holding a very weak hand but a hand that still might be the best hand or one that could become the best hand if an ace or a king hits the board. This means that if you bet in this spot, you are getting 9-to-1. If we ignore certain things, such as you may get raised, or you may get called but catch an ace or a king on fourth street that wins the pot for you, your bet needs to be successful about 10 percent of the time to break even.

When you are in this type of situation — and this type of situation occurs a great deal in hold'em — you should ask yourself how often you think your attempted bet will be successful. If your success rate is well below 10 percent, unless the game is extremely loose, I do not believe you can win playing hold'em. If it is about 10 percent, considering the fact that you may also get lucky and make the best hand some of the time that you are called or raised, your bet becomes moderately profitable. If you are successful a lot more than 10 percent of the time, then your bet becomes very profitable. In fact, being able to successfully get the pot a reasonable percentage of the time in this type of spot is one of the differences between those who win and those who do not.

If you are perceived by your opponents as a strong player, you should be able to make these types of semi-bluffs into very profitable bets. On the other hand, if you are considered to be a weak player, a loose player, or a wild player, these types of bets can become very costly for you. Worse, you may discover that some of your opponents, who will throw their hands away against someone else, might raise you when they have nothing and complete their resteal on fourth street, assuming that your card does not hit. Now your semi-bluff has become very expensive indeed. Yet I see constant advocation of an "image" that will put you into this type of situation. *Again, it is just plain wrong for games like hold'em and stud.* You do not want to encourage your opponents to make plays against you, especially the type of plays that will interfere with your winning strategy.

In closing, I want to emphasize that the ideas in this essay are very sophisticated and are just some of the weapons that the expert player keeps in his arsenal. To be successful at poker, you must be skilled in all aspects of the game, and image — that is, a tight but aggressive image in most forms of poker — is just one of those aspects. If you just play OK, or do only some things right, *don't expect to win.*

Image

Afterthought

As can be seen, my thoughts on image are definitely different from those of many other writers. One reason for this is that I believe poker is too complex for any one idea or concept to dominate winning play. Another reason is that I don't see many successful players, if I see any at all, who have the wild, crazy image that is often advocated.

In a way, this is a shame. It sure would be easier to "just put on my clown suit" and quickly rake in all the money.

Earlier in the text, I made a reference to playing seven-card stud with 60 mental pages. I suppose that image would probably be worth one-fourth to one-half a page. Not very much. Certainly not enough to make you into an automatic winner.

On the other hand, knowing which image is appropriate for the game you are in does have some merit. However, keep in mind that if you can't play, expect to go broke no matter how wonderful your image may be.

Part Six

Tournament Notes

Tournament Notes

Introduction

I have written a great deal on poker tournaments before. One of my books, *Gambling Theory and Other Topics*, contains a major section devoted to tournament strategy. But, as with many other aspects of poker, there are always a few loose ends to tie up.

The poker world includes a subculture of players known as "tournament junkies." I am not a member of this group. In fact, I don't particularly like to play tournaments for many reasons. One of them is that I don't always like to sit for a long period of time, especially when I get nothing in return. Another is that some of the survival strategies, which at times are correct in poker tournaments run counter to the way I want to gamble; that is, I like to seize the initiative. The idea of just sitting there hoping that other people will bust themselves out so I can "sneak" into a higher finish is not my idea of a dynamic gambler.

On the other hand, because of the different gambling mathematics that tournaments offer, they are fascinating to write about. This is true from both a practical and a theoretical point of view. Hence, we have this section. Let's get started.

Is Winning Everything?

As I have written many times before, correct tournament strategy for percentage-payback tournaments is somewhat different from standard ring-game strategy. In fact, in certain situations, especially late in a tournament, it can be a great deal different. But even though this is true, it is not exactly the purpose of this essay. The purpose is to discuss the differences between two types of successful tournament players. The first type plays in such a way that he maximizes his expectation, while the second type plays in such a way that he maximizes his probability of winning the event regardless of his expectation. Let's take a look at the differences between these two.

Suppose it is late in a tournament and there are just three players left. Players A and B each have a lot of chips, while Player C is behind but still has enough chips that the blinds and antes won't quickly wipe him out. Further, let's suppose that Player C is the type who will try to maximize his expectation. How will he play his hand?

There is only one strategy that he will follow. Player C will try to survive, hoping that Players A and B will get into a major confrontation and perhaps allow him to sneak into second place. Player C will try to take advantage of the fact that he profits due to percentage-payback mathematics when he is able to sit out the hand where the two big stacks go at it. (For more information on this subject see *Gambling Theory and Other Topics*.)

Now suppose that Player C is the type who will try to maximize his probability of winning the tournament. How will he play?

In this case there also is only one strategy that he will follow. Player C will try to get into a major confrontation with one of the two big stacks and hope to get lucky. If he does win the pot, he now will be in a position to win the tournament. Notice that he is not interested in sneaking into second place.

When gambling, it's clear that one usually should try to maximize his expectation. (The exception would be when the level of risk that an individual must assume becomes too great.) This means that the person who will try to sneak into second place will do better in the long run than the person who only wants to win the tournament. Could it be that the best tournament players don't win as many tournaments as some of the other regular tournament players? I think this statement might be true.

It also seems to me that some people who have become well-known because of their tournament wins actually may not deserve their fame. Obviously, however, if someone is good enough to win several tournaments, he must be doing some things right; in fact, I suspect that he is doing a lot of things right. But I can't help but wonder if there aren't a few people who are playing tournaments extremely well — and are winning more than their share of the money — yet who still are not that well-known to the poker-playing public.

I want to point out, however, that what I have just stated applies only to limit tournaments. A small number of players seem to win the majority of no-limit and pot-limit tournaments, because expert players in these games have a much greater edge over their weaker playing opponents than the experts at standard limit games. This is especially true if they are willing to make many rebuys.

In conclusion, when playing tournaments you should try to maximize your expectation. The exception might be if the "fame" of winning the tournament is so great that this alone dominates your decision. However, keep in mind that always trying to win the tournament will not be as profitable in the long run as the more conservative, alternate strategy.

Being an Alternate

It happens all the time: You try to enter a small buy-in poker tournament but don't get there in time. You are told that there isn't a seat for you but that if you would like to wait around and be an alternate, you will most likely get a chance to play. Is this a good move?

First, what exactly is an alternate? An alternate is someone who doesn't have a seat at the start of a tournament but who is allowed to buy-in during the rebuy period after someone else has gone broke and left. "At least you get to play," I have been told. But I've also heard "If you don't win a pot real fast, you don't have enough chips to stand a chance." In fact, most people that I have talked to feel that being an alternate is a bad deal, the kind of play that only a sucker would make. "You need chips to win a tournament, and how can you get chips if you are watching?"

One of the things I show in *Gambling Theory and Other Topics* is that in percentage-payback tournaments, the chips change value. Specifically, the more chips you have relative to the other players, the less each individual chip is worth, and the less chips you have relative to the other players, the more each individual chip is worth.

This important tournament concept has many impacts on your overall strategy. One of the most important is that in percentage-payback tournaments — and almost all tournaments today have this format — as long as you are broke and the rebuy is not progressive, it is a positive-expectation play. In other words, rebuying is correct and you should do it.

Here's an example. Suppose the rebuy to a tournament is $20. Wouldn't it be nice to get, let's say $22 worth of chips. Well, when you go broke in a poker tournament, this is exactly the sort of thing that happens. My advice is that if you are not prepared to rebuy five or six times, you probably shouldn't be in the tournament. This is because you will have to go into your survival mode while others who plan to rebuy can still play fast.

Now suppose you are an alternate. Isn't this the same as going broke and then rebuying? Of course it is. *Also, if it is a profitable play to rebuy when you are broke, wouldn't it also be a profitable play to be an alternate?* Absolutely. In fact, I would rather be an alternate than a regular player! Why enter a tournament at the beginning when I have no mathematical overlay, where by showing up late I immediately get one?

I'm sure that many of you are surprised by what I have just stated. But as I have pointed out, the conventional wisdom is just the opposite from what is really correct. Being an alternate is not a sucker play; the idea that you are being out-chipped before you sit down is wrong.

By the way, I'm assuming that all players in the tournament are equally skilled. If only excellent players are left — and this is extremely doubtful — then your rebuy or alternate buy-in might be incorrect. However, I have never seen a situation where I thought this was the case.

Finally, and I think this is where most people get confused, your chances of winning the tournament are reduced when you are an alternate because you have a smaller share of the chip pool. But, even though this is true, it has no impact on whether being an alternate is a good move or not.

Winner-Take-All Tournaments: Part I

What is the correct strategy for winner-take-all tournaments? Is it to play your normal best game, or should you try to survive? I recently read an argument for playing your normal best game, and this is the approach most people think is proper. But is it correct? Let's look at an example.

(By the way, winner-take-all tournaments are rare today though they used to be common many years ago. There is an exception: one-table satellites. For those who don't know, these are small tournaments usually held in conjunction with a major event where the winner of the satellite gains an entry into the main event.)

Suppose two players, call them A and B, agree to play a heads-up freeze-out. Further, let's assume that they each start with $1,000, that A is the better player, and that A has two strategies available to him. The first strategy wins at a rate of $10 an hour (in a typical game where the stakes are not escalated) but has a standard deviation very close to zero, while the second strategy wins at a much higher rate but has a standard deviation significantly larger than zero. (For those of you unfamiliar with the standard deviation, it is a statistical measure of the amount of short-term luck present in the game.)

Obviously, even though the second strategy would produce more money in the long run in a regular game, if the only thing Player A is interested in is the freeze-out (for example, suppose he will never play poker again or is totally unconcerned about what side games may be available), then clearly his best strategy for this tournament is to win at the lower rate. This is because he will virtually never lose, while the strategy that produces a higher win rate and would be the superior approach in a regular poker game will occasionally mean that player A will not leave the table with all the chips. This is the effect of a non-zero standard deviation.

This brings up an interesting question. Even though it seems obviously correct to adopt a survivalist strategy in tournaments, whether they are winner-take-all or percentage-payback, why do the most successful tournament players appear not to follow this approach? I believe there are of two reasons: The first has to do with the way chips change value (in percentage-payback tournaments), and the second has to do with the idea that it is correct to take advantage of tight play.

As I show in *Gambling Theory and Other Topics*, when prize money is awarded on a preset percentage for those few who outlast the rest of the field, the more chips you have, the less each individual chip is worth, and the less chips you have, the more each individual chip is worth. This has great implications on play, and at times — especially late in a tournament — it can make someone look as though he is playing wildly.

Taking advantage of tight play is also important because it allows you to steal lots of pots. I have seen tables develop in tournaments where the game has become so tight that raising every hand might not be bad as long as no one else has entered the pot. Of course, if someone else is already in, many normally playable hands should be quickly folded.

Returning to our original topic, do you play your normal best game, or should you try to survive in a winner-take-all tournament. I believe playing your normal best game is clearly wrong. Perhaps the better approach is trying to survive but also taking advantage of tight play, which may make your strategy look just the opposite to other players at the table. However, the chips won't change value in winner-take-all events as they do in regular tournaments, so the appropriate strategy changes that this concept normally triggers will not come into play. For example, attacking small stacks is now not as important.

Winner-Take-All
Tournaments: Part II

As the previous essay showed, trying to survive may be a better approach than playing your normal best game in a winner-take-all tournament. But is it the correct approach? Do you really want to just sit on your chips early in a one-table satellite? It turns out that there are two very strong arguments against this, one practical and one theoretical.

Practical Argument: For our survival approach to make sense, we assumed that the only poker of interest (to you) is the winner-take-all tournament. However, this is not realistic. Today, winner-take-all tournaments are pretty much limited to the one-table satellites spread at most major tournaments. If you are eliminated, you can rebuy into another satellite. For most players, this should change things dramatically. Now the emphasis should be less on surviving and more on maximizing your win rate, which in some cases might mean playing your normal best game.

I say "in some cases" because even in one-table satellites, many of your opponents will not play their normal best games. Many will play too tight. Some will play wildly, especially at the start. Others, once they get low on chips, will begin to play too loose because they are afraid that the blinds and antes will "eat them up." If your normal best game is capable of adjusting to these things, you should be in pretty good shape. Otherwise, you will need to play better than your normal best game.

Theoretical Argument: The reason for the survival approach was to reduce the standard deviation. (In many forms of gambling, reducing your standard deviation can be very important even if it also reduces your expectation a little. This is especially true if you are on a small bankroll.) This makes it more likely that you will win the tournament, even though it might take you a little longer to do so. But a problem develops when you try to reduce your standard deviation. Because of the escalating stakes, your standard deviation will always go up toward the end of the tournament since no matter how many chips you have, you will be in jeopardy. Consequently, you probably will be better off to reduce your standard deviation at the end of a tournament rather than at the beginning.

How do you do this? It's easy. Just get more chips and the higher betting limits won't put you in as much jeopardy. How do you get more chips? That's easy, too. Just gamble it up at the beginning of the tournament. Or, put another way, increase your standard deviation early.

Notice that this is a trade-off. The idea is to increase your standard deviation early but to reduce it later. This argument makes sense if the later decrease is much larger than the early increase, and I think this is the case.

Now this doesn't mean that you should play like a crazy person early on. Remember, you are still in a poker game, and you still must use your poker skills. But you should probably push all small edges to the maximum early in the tournament.

Conclusion: Trying to survive in a winner-take-all tournament is probably wrong, even though there are strong arguments supporting it. Playing your normal best game is also probably wrong, even though many individuals currently think this is the best approach. What one most likely should do is gamble it up — but not overdo it — early in a tournament and then settle down some depending on your chip position and who the remaining players are. In other words increase your standard deviation early and try to minimize it later. For those of you who prefer standard English as opposed to statistical terms, try to get lucky early but play solid once there are just a small number of players left.

One final comment: Even though the rake on one-table satellites appears high, I believe they are very profitable for a few people who regularly play them. Put another way, these small, winner-take-all tournaments are well worth playing, providing that you use the right strategy.

Two Tournament Mistakes

Correct strategy in tournaments can be very different from what is correct in regular play. Many players understand this, but what they fail to understand is how dramatic these differences are.

What follows are two examples of misplayed hands in tournaments. What is interesting is that both hands would have been played correctly in a ring game, and they both represent a very powerful poker tournament concept. The game in both cases is no-limit hold'em.

The first play was made by a friend of mine. He held two aces and was against a player he knew very well, plus he was sure that his opponent also held a pair, but not a very large one. The flop contained three unrelated cards and my friend decided to bet half his money. The reason he gave for this was, "If I bet half my money on the flop, I was sure to get a call, and then I could get the rest of it in on the turn and most likely be called again. However, if I bet all my money on the flop, I might not be called at all." Well, the hand was played just as my friend had foreseen except that a six was the river card, and the winning hand was a set of sixes, not a pair of aces as was expected.

The second play supposedly occurred during the championship event of the 1990 World Series of Poker. (I heard about it a few days later from someone still complaining about his bad beat.) A late-position player with about $25,000 in chips held a pair of threes and raised $4,000. The player in the big blind, who also had about $25,000 in chips, held a pair of kings. He called the $4,000 and then raised an additional $4,000. The person who held the pair of threes now went all in (in a vain attempt to steal the pot) and found himself trapped. Unfortunately for the holder of the kings, a three came on the turn and he found himself out of the tournament.

Both of these hands sound like bad beats and they would be in a regular game. In fact, in a regular game, both hands would have been played brilliantly — even though they lost — since they maximize the expectation for the player holding the big pair. But in a tournament, things can be very different.

The reason for this is the escalating stakes that occur in tournaments. Unless you win a lot of pots, your chips are always in jeopardy, and one bad hand can and often will put you on the sidelines. Consequently, if you don't shut your opponent out of the pot, there is a good chance that you cannot recover from those times that he does draw out on you. In a regular game, even though you don't particularly like it, you can reach into your pocket, purchase some more chips, and perhaps still have a good win. But in a tournament, unless it is still during the rebuy period, this is not true.

Notice that we have given two extreme examples of hands that represent an important tournament concept: *Try to win pots without a showdown.* Put another way, you need an exceptionally strong hand to give your opponent a chance to play bad. If this means giving up some of your expected value in exchange for winning the pot more often, then this is how the hand should usually be played.

Now for a final example. Several years ago, another friend of mine — who is also one of the best players around — was in the running for the most valuable player award at a major tournament. In the no-limit hold'em event, he was dealt a pair of aces. A couple of players had already called, and my friend moved all in. Nothing unusual about this, but at the same time, he turned his aces face up on the table. He correctly wanted to make sure that no one would call him. Many people who either saw or heard about this play thought my friend was crazy. But given the fact that he was in the running for a significant most valuable player prize, as well as possibly winning the particular event, his play was clearly correct.

In fact, I consider this to be the best poker play of all time. The tournament director announced a change in the rules shortly after this play was made. The rule change stated that anyone who exposed his cards during the play of the hand would forfeit the pot. This should give you an idea of how powerful this concept is.

Taking Advantage of Tight Play

In *Gambling Theory and Other Topics*, I have a section on poker tournament strategy. One of the concepts I give is to take advantage of tight play. *In many ways, this is the most important idea that exists in tournament play, especially late in an event.* However, many people who play tournaments seem to be completely unaware of this concept.

Ironically, this idea should not even exist. Most of your typical opponents will play too tight, and there is no strategic reason for them to do so. Why they play too tight is because if you go broke in a tournament, with the exception of during the rebuy period, you are out. And most people don't like to leave a poker game early, especially if they are broke.

When your opponents are playing too tight, you obviously should try to steal more often if no one has entered the pot, but also you should be less inclined to call with medium-strength hands if the pot has already been opened. In addition, keep in mind that your drawing hands have gone down in value. If you make a flush for example, you will have fewer opponents to collect from, plus the ones you are up against will probably be less likely to pay you off. Finally, if you correctly pick your spots, your bluffs will be more successful, but betting for value should only be done with reasonably good hands.

There are, of course, some exceptions to this general strategy. First, even though the typical player does tend to tighten his play in a tournament, there always will be a few opponents who do not.

Second, if you are playing in a tournament that allows rebuys, many of your opponents will play very loosely during the rebuy period because going broke will not send them home. Keep in mind that it is much less likely for someone who does not intend to rebuy to be playing loose (he is already in his survival mode) than it is for someone who is prepared to rebuy several times. Knowing who does — and who does not — intend to rebuy at your table should significantly impact your strategy.

Third, many tournament participants do not tighten up until they perceive the stakes as a threat to their stacks. Let me give a specific example. Suppose you are given $500 in tournament chips, and the starting limit is $15-$30. Many of your opponents won't perceive this limit as a threat to their stacks; consequently, they won't adjust their play. In fact, they may play extra loose. However, at the $30-$60 limit this may not be the case anymore. Now those same opponents who were playing extremely loose, even if they could not rebuy, may begin to play very tight. When this happens, you also need to adjust your play. It may even be hard to believe that you are sitting at the same table just after the limits have increased. (By the way, I am not saying that the $15-$30 limit is no threat to $500 while $30-$60 limit is, but that many of your opponents will react in this fashion whether it is correct or not.)

There is much more to tournament strategy, especially late in an event, than just this one idea. For a detailed discussion, I recommend my book *Gambling Theory and Other Topics*, as well as *Sklansky on Poker*, which includes a section on tournament play. These are the only sources for tournament strategy that I think are completely accurate.

In conclusion, let me note that the strategy discussed in this essay is more effective in small tournaments where the majority of entrants are not expert players. In large major tournaments that contain many highly skilled players, a bigger percentage of your opponents understand this idea. However, it still should influence your play simply because enough of your opponents play exactly as I have described.

Getting Them All-In

A poker acquaintance of mine recently finished second in a major hold'em tournament. When it got down to two players, an interesting hand came up. Our hero was on the button, had a big stack, and had picked up two aces. His opponent, who now was the big blind, had many fewer chips than my friend. The question now arises, should the player on the button, who held the aces, have raised or just called?

Even though some of you might think the answer is obvious, it really isn't. This is one of those situations where you must play poker well to gain the maximum. Let's suppose that you have the two aces. Clearly, you want your opponent to go all in. There are two reasons for this: First, two aces have the best of it against any other hand, and second, because of the percentage paybacks that most tournaments today offer, the value of each individual chip depends on how many chips you happen to have. Specifically, the more chips you have, the less each individual chip is worth, and the less chips that you have, the more each individual chip is worth. This means that since the person in the big blind has the smallest stack, it will theoretically cost him more to go all in than it will cost you — the person with the two aces — to set him all in, even though each of you will put into the pot the same amount in chips.

So what is the answer? It depends on which move — raising or just calling — is more likely to get your opponent to go all in. If you think your opponent will over defend his blind, go ahead and raise. This is especially likely if he is on a short stack and if you think that he now believes that the blinds are a threat to his survival. On the other hand, if your opponent perceives you as a tight player who will raise only with strong hands, which means that he may be quick to throw his hand away, calling is clearly best. Another possibility is that your opponent is very aggressive. This means if you just limp in, he may be likely to raise, which will allow you to reraise. Obviously, if this is the case, you should probably call. This may even be true if you think it is likely that your opponent will call your raise. There are also many other possibilities, but as you can see, you must play poker well to maximize your expectation in this situation.

Now suppose the situation is sort of reversed: that is, you are the short stack, are on the button, but have the two aces. Should you raise or just call? Again, you need to consider many of the ideas that we just talked about, but it is now more likely for the raise to be correct since it will cost your opponent less to put you all in than it will cost you. Remember, the chips change value, so your opponent should be willing to do this even with a hand that he figures would be taking a little the worse of it if you were not in a tournament.

In fact, we have just touched upon an important tournament concept: *It is correct late in a tournament to call very liberally if (1) you have good chip position, (2) it won't cost much to call, and (3) you have an opportunity to eliminate this opponent.* Failure to take advantage of this strategy can prove very costly to those of you who play a lot of tournaments.

By the way, if you are wondering how my friend did. He raised with the two aces, was called, lost the pot, and did not win the tournament.

Small Tournaments:
Are They Right For You?

Are small tournaments worth playing? Is the monetary return they offer to skilled players worth the time that it takes to play them? And most important, what if you are on a short bankroll? Are small tournaments a good investment to those of you who are close to standing on the rail? I recently read the following statement by another poker writer:

> The potential return on a buy-in often far exceeds what would be a realistic return on an investment in a live game. A $25 buy-in tournament with only 15 or 20 players may carry more than $1,000 first-place prize money, which is almost impossible to win at the table in a few hours with a $25 buy-in.

Obviously this statement is correct. There is no question that tournaments, whether large or small, offer a significant return on your money if you should happen to get lucky and win. This is the primary reason why they have become so popular. But the statement I quoted also seems to indicate that small tournaments are a good investment for those on a small bankroll. Is this true? If you are virtually broke, are you better off in these events as opposed to playing in the little games?

In *Gambling Theory and Other Topics*, one of the most important ideas I present is that the skillful gambler tries to balance his bankroll against his expectation (win rate) and the standard deviation (the statistical measurement of short-term luck), which will allow his bankroll to grow in an optimal fashion. This means that if your bankroll is small, you need to play in games where your expected win rate is relatively high and the standard deviation is relatively low. If you consistently violate this rule, there is a high probability that you will go broke. (By the way, violation of this rule keeps a great many otherwise skilled players on the rail.)

Does a tournament fit this criteria? In other words, can you have a high win rate and a small standard deviation in these events? Are they a good investment if you currently are struggling to come up with a buy-in? The answer is, probably not.

I do believe that if you play tournaments extremely well, you may have a relatively high win rate. But virtually all tournaments also have a large luck factor. (Haven't you heard the statement "anyone can win.") This is especially true of small events that allow rebuys and quickly raise the stakes, and almost all small tournaments I know of have this type of format. Even though you may expect to do well in the long run, they are no place for those of you with small bankrolls. Remember, it may take a very long time to get into the long run. (In addition, the rebuys can make these tournaments much more expensive than they first appear. And keep in mind that if you do go broke, it is correct to rebuy.)

Of course, this doesn't mean that most readers should quit playing tournaments. I agree that they can be a lot of fun, and I am not trying to discourage any cardroom from promoting them. My comments are directed only to those of you who are trying to survive. Stick to the sure thing. It's true that a couple of tournament wins may set you on the path to riches, but if your bankroll is not anywhere close to where you would like it, stay in the ring games.

Are Poker Tournaments Dying?

Poker tournaments seem to be bigger and better than ever. With the phenomenal growth of the "World Series of Poker" and the massive proliferation of many other tournaments, it appears to the uneducated eye that tournament poker is the wave of the future. In fact there have been poker tournaments in places like Louisiana, and you can even take a luxury cruise and participate in some form of competition. But I suspect that things are not as they appear.

The reason I say this is that several major tournaments are no longer with us, including those at the Frontier, the Tropicana, the Riviera, the Stardust, the Golden Nugget, the Las Vegas Hilton, Caesar's Tahoe, and most recently Caesar's Palace. It seems strange that this has happened since poker tournaments set new attendance records every year. In fact, the newest major tournament, the "Diamond Jim Brady" held annually at the Bicycle Club in Bell Gardens, California, has become a spectacular success. So what is going on? Why have some of these poker tournaments been discontinued?

I suspect that the reasons are complex and many, but one I never see mentioned in print is that major poker tournaments are quite costly to the casinos that operate and promote them. How is this possible? Don't these events attract a lot of people who otherwise might not venture into the casino? And aren't tournaments getting bigger and better every year?

All this is true. However, when I say costly, I'm not referring to the actual expense of the tournament itself but to the action that the casino loses. I've always been told that the additional people these tournaments bring in means that the action increases at the other casino games. But is this really the case? Does a casino make more money when it has to take out 20 or 30 blackjack tables to accommodate lots of poker players? And as for the increased action, is it really the type of action that most casinos want?

200

Another thing never mentioned is that today's successful poker player is different from his predecessor. The successful old-time player was more instinctive in nature; he learned to become a good player only after many years of gambling. But today's best players are more mathematical and scientific in their approach to the game. In addition, there are several good books available that help these players quantify that approach, meaning that it does not take as long to reach a high level of skill as it used to. The vast majority of money won in today's game is won by this new breed, not by the few old-time players who are still around.

So what does this have to do with whether a poker tournament is the type of thing a casino would want? It has a lot to do with it, because the very characteristics that make a modern winning poker player are carried to the casino's other games. For instance, today's "smart" player does not spend a lot of time at the craps table like his predecessor used to. And if he does play craps, he will make only the very best bets and is sure to get the majority of his money on the table by taking the odds, one of the few "free" bets casinos offer.

And, when it comes to blackjack, many of today's new breed can count cards or at least can play a virtually perfect basic strategy. So if one of them gets into action at the blackjack table, the casino may actually lose money. In addition, you will never see one of these smart players sitting at a roulette wheel, and if he makes a sports bet, he is probably trying to "middle" the casino.

I could go on, but I suspect that when the casino hosting a major poker tournament examines its bottom line, in some cases it may not look so good. Sure, there were big crowds, and sure, lots of rooms were booked. And to the uneducated eye, the tournament appeared to be a huge success, and many of them probably were. But to top casino management, things may not look so great. Casinos are in the business of attracting people to gamble at their tables. There was a time when those who participated in poker tournaments also spent many hours at the gaming tables, but I wonder if this is true today.

I suspect that as years go by, there will be fewer major tournaments at Nevada casinos, especially at those houses that understand the increased action tournaments supply actually may be detrimental to their bottom line. However, more major tournaments may appear at places like the Bicycle Club in California where casino gambling is not legal, even though games like pai gow poker and super pan nine are spread. But as far as Nevada is concerned, the great poker tournament boom is, in my opinion, past its peak, although a few events, like "The World Series of Poker," are spectacular successes and probably will continue to be so.

The Demise of
Semi-Legal Tournaments

A phenomenon that began several years ago is what I refer to as "semi-legal tournaments." These are tournaments held in out-of-state locations where poker and most other forms of gambling are normally illegal. Even though many of these events received a lot of publicity and were well attended, most never got off the ground. There was, however, one major exception: the "Cajun Cup," which was held in Louisiana. It not only got off the ground, but also ran for four years and was very successful until it was finally closed down.

Many skilled players from Nevada and elsewhere looked forward to these events because the side games were extremely good. Several people told me that the middle-limit hold'em games at the "Cajun Cup" were some of the best games they had ever seen. In addition, many players could combine a nice vacation with an expected win. No wonder so many people wanted to go to these events.

Although I never attended the "Cajun Cup," I am under the impression that it was run honestly and efficiently. The only complaint I ever heard was that the collection and rakes were a bit too high. Still, I can't help but think that the potential for abuse at a semi-legal tournament somewhere would be too tempting for some people to resist. Think about it. Would you feel as secure playing poker in some hotel ballroom located halfway across the United States as you do in places like Binion's Horseshoe or the Mirage in Las Vegas, or at the Bicycle Club or the Commerce Club in California?

In *Gambling and The Law* Professor I. Nelson Rose points out that the history of gambling shows that gambling almost always will become corrupt unless it is closely regulated, and that this corruption in the past has forced the government to step in and put a stop to most gambling activities. This is why there was almost no legal gambling in this country in the early 1900s.

Of course corruption has not occurred in Nevada or Atlantic City. In fact gambling seems to expand in these places every year, and I believe one reason for this is that the games are well-regulated. As a result, the chances of being cheated are kept to a minimum.

This brings up another point. Even if the individuals promoting and running the semi-legal tournaments are 100-percent honest, will they be able to ensure the integrity of the games. This is done in most major cardrooms through the use of high-quality surveillance equipment and by well-trained floor personnel. Much of this equipment won't be available in some out-of-state hotel, and the quality of personnel working the floor may not be equivalent to what serious poker players are used to.

So what's the bottom line? In my opinion, it is probably for the best that these tournaments are most likely no longer with us. Even though the games may have been great, I think in the long run we are much better off attending tournaments like "The World Series of Poker" and "The L.A. Open." Besides, the side action is also great at these major events.

Improving Tournaments

I dislike poker tournaments and rarely play in them for several reasons. First, the element of luck is very large in tournaments, minimizing the skill factor. Second, you have to sit for long periods of time, which I don't always like to do and find very frustrating. And third, I think a lot of tournaments could be run much better, which brings me to the purpose of this essay. Following are some suggestions that I hope tournament directors will consider implementing in the future as I believe they would greatly improve many events.

Suggestion No. 1: Change the money distribution. One problem with tournaments is that usually too much money goes to the winner. This can be easily remedied by giving less money to first place and more money to those who finish second and lower.

So what's wrong with giving first place too much money? Plenty. To begin with, it stops the competition at the final table because the players left often make deals dividing up the money. Now suppose you have a big crowd watching. Since the money and perhaps even the positions are already decided, spectators are treated to just one stupid play after another as the final few participants are now merely interested in getting it over with.

A second problem with the current money distribution is that it makes tournaments too much of a long shot for the skilled player. Remember, even if you have the best of it, it still may not be a good bet if your risk is too high. This is especially true if you are on a small bankroll.

And finally, the current money distribution causes many plays, especially those made late in a tournament, to be very survival-oriented. It seems to me that the correct way to play poker is to extract the maximum amount from your opponents. *Punish them every time you have a small edge.* Put another way, force them to pay dearly for any mistake they might make.

However, in a tournament — especially late in the game — depending on your chip position, the chip position of your opponents, and how the money is distributed, the best strategy on a particular hand is sometimes the equivalent of running and hiding. I believe the best poker players should win the tournaments, not those who are best at this very different game.

Suggestion No. 2: Slow the chip escalation toward the end of the tournament. I have already mentioned that one reason I dislike tournaments is that they are too luck-oriented. The major cause of this is the constant chip escalation. With big fields, it is hard for tournament directors to do otherwise, but the problem is especially acute toward the end of many tournaments. This seems to be the most common complaint that players have.

It appears that some tournament directors want participants to feel that they got their money's worth but also want to get things over with. This translates into reasonable starting stacks for the first limit but quick escalation of the limits once there are just a couple of tables left. What this does is greatly reduce the skill factor, and when the tournament reaches its most crucial point, it becomes a crap shoot. I've even seen tournaments with four or five players remaining where no one had enough chips left to make a bet on every betting round for just one hand.

If anything, the escalation of stakes should be slowed down toward the end of an event to give players a chance to show who really is the best poker player in town. However, I know of only a few tournaments where this is done.

Suggestion No. 3: Take position into account when someone is moved to another table. Specifically, I am referring to keeping tables balanced with an equal number of people during tournament play. I agree that this should be done. But at virtually every tournament I have seen, when a table goes short, it is either broken or someone from another table is immediately added. The trouble with this procedure is that it sometimes forces players to take a blind twice in a row. In a hold'em tournament, for instance, how many of you have been forced to move to another table where you must take your big blind just after you've already taken your big blind?

What's wrong with this? Well, if you are not in the best of chip positions, especially late in a tournament, then being forced to take an extra blind can easily destroy your chances of a good finish since the blind may require a significant portion of your chips. The obvious solution to this problem is that when you are moved to another table but have just taken your blind, then you should be allowed to wait for the blind to go past you before receiving a hand.

Suggestion No. 4: Stop encouraging large tokes. I know this suggestion will be controversial, but exactly why should someone who has just hit a 100-to-1 shot be encouraged — expected — to toke big? The problem with this is that large tokes, plus taxes, may eliminate the overlay that the skilled player has in tournaments, making them unattractive to many players. The solution is to let some of the juice go to the dealers.

I agree that dealers have the right to make a decent wage for working at tournaments. But I don't think that the person who is lucky enough to win the tournament should bear most of the burden. If it is necessary to increase the juice to ensure that dealers are treated fairly, then I am in favor of doing this. In fact, I would support the idea of a higher entry fee if no tipping was allowed, provided that a fair portion of the higher fee went to the dealers, floor people, and other tournament personnel.

Suggestion No. 5: Eliminate rebuys from major tournaments.
It can easily be shown that in percentage payback tournaments, if you have gone broke, it is always correct to rebuy as long as the rebuy is not progressive. This being the case, rebuys favor those people with large bankrolls since they can play more aggressively and take more chances during the rebuy period. Consequently, rebuy tournaments don't favor the best players, but instead favor the richest players and perhaps the more reckless players. Because

of this, I think that rebuys should not be allowed in the major tournaments, especially those with a lot of prestige.

Final note: I wish to thank a specific world-class player, whose name I will not mention, for coming to me with some of these ideas, and I hope this essay will start the process for making tournaments better for all of us.

Tournament Notes

Afterthought

I hope I've been able to take care of most of the loose ends with this section. I suspect however that new things will pop up in the future that I did not address.

As can be seen, playing correctly in a tournament is very complicated. In fact, I think correct tournament strategy is significantly tougher than correct ring-game strategy. This is because the chips change value, and you need to be conscious not only of the correct normal poker strategy, but also of how you should adjust that strategy based on your chip position, the payoffs for the different places, how tight your opponents are playing, and so forth.

Another thing the reader should remember is that running a tournament, especially a major event, is a very complicated task. Those people who have made these contests successful deserve our thanks. Events like the "World Series of Poker" have done a great deal toward promoting the game and I'm confident that they will continue to do so.

Part Seven

In the Cardrooms

In the Cardrooms

Introduction

Knowing how to play your hands well doesn't do much good if you don't have good games to play in. Good games appear because of many things. One of which is a well-run cardroom that treats its customers right. However, providing this type of environment is not always easy to do as some poker players at times misbehave.

In my opinion, most cardrooms that exist today are well-run. Those that are not usually don't stay in business. Sometimes a poorly run room will do quite well for an extended period of time. However, as soon as some competition appears, its business quickly vanishes.

At the time of this writing, there used to be six major cardrooms in Gardena, California. Today, there are two. The highly successful room in Bell, California, is also no more, and two major cardrooms in Las Vegas have recently collapsed.

I'm sure that there are many reasons these rooms fared poorly, and I don't claim to be an expert on their problems. But I did play in all of them, and one thing that came across was that most of these rooms could have treated their customers much differently.

Cardrooms and The Pros

One topic that I have never seen anything written about is the relationship between cardrooms and the professional poker players who frequent them. This is a unique relationship in the world of casino gambling, because this is the only group of gamblers who are usually expected to win but who are also welcomed by the house.

The professional poker players who regularly visit casinos are the glue that keep many cardrooms thriving. By always being there, by helping to start games, and by keeping the games going, these pros ensure a pretty nice drop for cardrooms that build their games around them. (Some cardrooms hire shills and/or props to perform these functions, but in my opinion, the best places to play poker do not incur this expense.)

But this relationship is not always a smooth one. Professional poker players can cause problems for the casinos. To begin with, the pros might win money from a hotel guest that the pit expects to get. In fact, if a tourist plays poorly, and this is often the case, he may lose his money much faster at the poker table than he would if he were playing craps or blackjack. This is especially true if he plays in a high-stakes game where the competition is more likely to be tough.

Even worse is that local poker experts are not always known to treat their poor-playing opponents well. What happens is that in poker, as in almost all forms of gambling, the short-term luck factor is very large. This means that excellent players can, and will, have some nights when they are significant losers, and the poor-playing tourist, who gets lucky in some pot, is then chastised and lectured by the expert. Sometimes the tourist becomes so insulted that the casino may lose a future customer or its current customer may no longer find himself in a gambling mood.

This is a real concern for any casino. It is true that poker rooms can earn their share, but casinos must make sure that cardrooms are

214 Part Seven: In the Cardrooms

not costly in other ways. If this means disciplining some of their regulars every now and then, it should be done.

In addition, some poker pros look and dress like bums. As ridiculous as it might sound, I have always wondered why more cardrooms have never experimented with a dress code. This would be especially appropriate in those casinos claiming to be "class acts."

However, all this being said, the professional player does expect, and should insist on, a well-run room. In fact, for many so-called pros to survive, there are a number of essential things that a poker room needs to do.

First, a cardroom must hire competent floor people who are able to make consistent yet accurate decisions quickly. In addition, floor personnel must make players, especially visitors from out of town, feel comfortable and at home playing poker. This can easily be done by presenting a pleasant and friendly attitude. Personnel who are too busy to put someone's name on a list or who take their time when settling a dispute at the table should not be allowed to work the floor.

Second, an expedient and simple set of rules is absolutely necessary. This will ensure that the decision-making process doesn't get bogged down because floor personnel can't remember all the rules. Trying to have rules that cover every possible situation sounds like a good idea, but there is always someone who will find an exception and will not only "pull a shot" but slow the game down as well.

Third, top management people need to spend a reasonable amount of time in the poker room so they will have a good handle on any problems the room may have. In my experience, those cardrooms that are run the poorest are also the cardrooms where no one ever sees the manager. I do recognize that the cardroom manager has more to do than just watch poker games, but watching those games at least a few hours a week is essential.

Fourth, professional players need competent and professional dealers who (1) deal out a lot of hands, (2) can quickly and accurately read the board once all the cards are exposed, and (3) minimize their talking and, of course, do not analyze hands that are played. Also, dealers should do just that, deal. Their responsibilities should not include telling players how to behave or making decisions, and they should not deal any games that they are unfamiliar with.

Once in a major Las Vegas cardroom, I was playing in the biggest game that was currently being spread. When it came time to change dealers, I was amazed that our new dealer was the chip runner who, as far as I knew, had never dealt before. The best cardrooms use their best dealers for their biggest games. Putting break-in dealers at the medium and high limits can be a disaster, not only for the players but for the novice dealers as well.

Another important thing professional players need in a cardroom is a good system to "brush" players into the game. This may mean that the games the professionals play must be put on the rail and that the brush, besides encouraging onlookers to play, must be able to quickly explain the game and make it sound attractive. It also may be necessary to provide a host for some particular game. If this is the case, the cardroom needs to make sure that the host is friendly and spends a good deal of time talking to the players. In my opinion, rooms that hire hosts who never speak to their regular pros do not really want the games.

One of the reasons a good brush is so important is that most poker pros do not play that well. While it's true that a small number of people have made a lot of money playing poker, most of those who attempt to play for a living go broke. They either can't win enough to cover their expenses or they don't play nearly as well as they think they do. Put another way, if a cardroom doesn't get some "producers" in its games every now and then, it may not have as many games in the future.

Finally, I'm reminded of an incident that occurred in a southern California cardroom a few years ago. I walked into the club early in the morning and sat in what looked like a pretty good short-handed game. The game appeared attractive because there was one well known "live" player sitting at the table. Also, since it was early in the morning, there were a lot of empty tables in the facility. After I had taken my seat, the floorman came up and announced that he was moving the game to the other side of the room. Upon hearing this, our live player announced that she had been playing for 24 hours, and if she was going to have to get up, she would go home. "I guess you'll have to go home then," came the reply, and of course, without her, the game quickly broke. Needless to say, this is one of those situations that I've been talking about. This floorman was not concerned with keeping the game going and did not care at all about the needs of professional poker players. He not only cost us expected profit, but managed to reduce the cardroom's drop as well.

The Collapse of
Two Cardrooms

Two major Las Vegas cardrooms recently collapsed. Even though these were places where a lot of people at one time or another played poker, both rooms eventually lost their business. Why did this occur? What happened that made two formerly very successful operations fail? What do rooms need to do to stop this potentially bad trend?

First, we need to understand why these two rooms collapsed. Even though both were located at large first-class casinos, I believe their troubles were the result of treating their customers poorly. And when the local poker players found other places to play, they deserted these rooms. If a poker room does not have a core of regulars to start games and keep them going, the room at best will have only a small number of games. This means that the room won't have a worthwhile drop, and if it doesn't have a worthwhile drop, then good-bye cardroom.

What is interesting, however is that these two cardrooms treated their customers poorly in very different ways. In my opinion, the first room seemed to have the attitude that it didn't want anyone to win. Perhaps top casino management was afraid that we poker players would take winnings away from the pit. Perhaps a few people in charge of the cardroom were failed poker players and were jealous of those successful pros who could do well at the game. Perhaps the negative attitude was for some other reason. But many things were done, whether intentionally or not, to discourage games.

As an example, when players wanted to raise the stakes, their request was usually denied. The middle-limit games were kept far away from the rail, making it more difficult to brush in tourists. The room had so many rules that games often would get bogged down in a ridiculous decision-making process that turned many customers off. (In fact, many local players thought the rules were interpreted in such a way that unfair decisions often were made against them in favor of "hotel guests." Other players believed the rules made the room too restrictive.) Break-in dealers often found themselves dealing in the bigger games. The code of conduct that was enforced was way too strict. As one player said to me, "Playing poker there is like going to church." Small games were promoted with giveaways, while middle-limit games were neglected. And finally, players complaints seemed to fall on deaf ears.

The other room failed, again in my opinion, because management and staff could not care less how their customers were treated. For instance, a player often would have to wait five to 10 minutes before the brush would even write his name on the list. If the player got tired of waiting and wrote his name down himself, it usually would be crossed off. New games would be called down, but there would be no dealers or chips available to get them started. Consequently, after another five- or 10-minute wait, many of the players would leave. The floor personnel never seemed to want to make a decision. In fact, one night when there was a major dispute at my table, the floorman announced that when the yelling stopped, he would make his decision. He promptly wandered off, and the dispute continued. In addition, very little effort was made to spread a variety of games. Even so, this was still a very successful cardroom — until another game became available in a room where customers were treated extremely well.

I think that many cardroom managers and potential cardroom managers could benefit by observing the operation of some of the more successful cardrooms. These include the Mirage and Binion's Horseshoe in Las Vegas and the Commerce Club and Bay 101 in California. In my opinion, these rooms are successful because they treat their customers right.

Where are the Big Games?

A lot of poker players like to play big. When I say "big," I'm referring to games at the $30-$60 level or higher; when I say "higher," I'm speaking of games up to and beyond $300-$600. But in Las Vegas and elsewhere throughout Nevada, these games virtually do not exist. The only exceptions are in the poker room at the Mirage where these games are regularly spread, and in the cardroom at Binion's Horseshoe where occasionally some bigger games do get down.

Big games, of course are spread during the major tournaments in Nevada. But many participants in these games are the same Nevada players who regularly play much smaller throughout the rest of the year. A lot of them, if given the opportunity, would prefer to play bigger at other times. But few big games are available on a regular basis.

This seems kind of strange, especially when you consider how much money can be wagered on other casino games. For example, one major Las Vegas casino will not allow a bet at the poker table larger than $8, and this bet is allowed only on the last round of play. Yet at the blackjack tables, you are permitted to make bets into the thousands of dollars. This casino is not an exception. The poker action it allows is typical of the action most casinos in Nevada will tolerate at their poker tables.

In California, this is not the case. Lots of bigger games are spread in many cardrooms, and these cardrooms have been spreading these games for years. Why is this? Are there bigger bankrolls in Los Angeles and San Francisco? Do bigger games reflect the larger population that California cardrooms have to draw from? Do players on the West Coast have more nerve than their Nevada counterparts? Or is there another reason why California cardrooms regularly spread big games and Nevada casinos do not?

Suppose you are a casino executive. A main function of your job is to make sure that your casino is as profitable as possible, which seems to infer that you should make your customers as happy as possible. Why then can't poker players have higher-stakes games? Because a casino executive also must look at the bottom line and must consider the impact that large poker games may have on the rest of the casino and its patrons. And here is where I believe the problem lies.

The typical Las Vegas tourist is a middle-income person who is just here to have some fun. He is not wealthy. Depending on the casino he is visiting, he may have a few hundred dollars or a couple of thousand dollars in his pocket to gamble with. Now suppose this person sits down in, let's say, a $30-$60 hold'em game. (I'm assuming that this game exists. Normally, there is no cardroom in Nevada that regularly spreads a hold'em game of this size.)[5] If he has little conception of how to play — and this is common for many out-of-towners who sit in the middle-stakes hold'em games — and if the game is reasonably tough, his loss rate will generally average between $200 and $400 an hour. Compare this to playing blackjack where the same tourist averages $50 bets. (By the way, most tourists don't bet this much at the blackjack tables.) Now his loss rate will be between $40 and $80 an hour. (These blackjack figures are correct, even though huge numbers have at times appeared in the blackjack literature. The figures I used are based on a recent paper given by blackjack authority Peter Griffin.) This is quite a difference.

Consequently, if the tourist chooses to play medium-stakes hold'em instead of blackjack, the poker players will win money that the casino expects to get. In addition, the tourist will go broke quickly. He may be mad at the casino for allowing him to get caught in this trap, and he might even find his vacation ruined. Worse, the tourist may never return to this casino. *Thus it appears that the casino loses money in two ways: It has an immediate short-term loss when the poker experts clean out one of its customers, and it*

---

[5]The Mirage is now spreading hold'em games this large on a regular basis.

has a long-term loss if this particular tourist decides not to come back.

However, this is not the whole story. What do poker players do with the money they have won? Do they stash it away never to be seen again? Do they invest it wisely? Or do they go on wild spending sprees? No, they give a good portion of the money they win back to the casinos.

Most poker players I know are gamblers. They constantly bet sports and occasionally can be found in the pit, especially on an off night when they find themselves "stuck." It's true that some poker players have become very wealthy. But many more go broke than are successful, and in my opinion, the casinos get their fair share from these people.

Casinos have had a negative attitude toward expert blackjack players ever since winning blackjack strategies were first produced in the early 1960s. I believe this same attitude may be beginning to appear in the poker world. Of course, some Nevada casinos, like Binion's Horseshoe and the Mirage (there are also others) treat their poker players great. Other casinos however, seem to have a more negative attitude toward serious poker experts. I hope this proves to be only a passing trend.

Are Cardrooms
Really Unprofitable?

I recently read an argument defending cardrooms that are going to higher rakes. Apparently, cardrooms don't make enough money when compared to the rest of the casino to justify their existence unless the rakes are increases. I, for one, don't buy this argument.

Suppose you are playing $10-$20 hold'em in a Las Vegas cardroom. This means that you usually are paying a maximum of $2 which translates into a drop of about $60 per hour for the casino, assuming that the dealer puts out a reasonable number of hands. Now suppose the game runs for an average of 16 to 17 hours per day. Then the drop for this game is approximately $1,000 per day, which is more than $350,000 per year. Not bad for a very small piece of real estate, especially since poker tables are not supposed to make any money. Moreover, games like $1-$4 stud, where the rake is much higher, will produce an even larger drop.

But the claim is that poker does not produce as much money as other casino games. Well, let's look at blackjack. Everyone agrees that blackjack is very profitable. If it wasn't, there wouldn't be so many blackjack tables around.

But how much money does a blackjack table make? Since I don't have access to casino figures, I can only speculate. First, the typical blackjack player losses at a rate of about 1½ percent, not the 6 percent figure that is often quoted. (This was shown in a recent paper by blackjack authority Peter Griffin.) Let's assume that there are four players at the table, each averaging $10 per bet and each playing about 100 hands per hour. This means that their total action is approximately $4,000 per hour, and a 1½ percent advantage for the casino produces a hold of about $60.

In this made-up example, it appears that blackjack has about the same money-making ability for the casino as its poker games. I recognize that there are differences my example ignores. For instance, a casino will have a much greater expectation against a high roller at the blackjack table than from the time fees it will collect at a big poker game. On the other hand, I think a successful poker room does (and should) improve the casino's bottom line.

I want to state that I believe a casino does have the right to make a reasonable profit from its poker games. After all, the casino not only supplies a service, but also makes an effort to keep its games clean and efficiently run. In addition, California cardrooms that charge more than their Nevada counterparts for playing poker have the right to do so as expenses in California are much higher. However, I also think you are a bit naive if you swallow the argument that poker rooms at major casinos are not profitable.

Finally, I want to mention an argument that I observed several years ago in a large, southern California cardroom between a floorman and a troublemaker who regularly played in the big games. "Sir," the floorman said, "you can't behave like that in this cardroom." "Listen buddy," the troublemaker replied, "when you pay $50,000 a year in collections, you can behave anyway you want."

Some Cardroom Suggestions

Most cardrooms are well-run. A few, of course, are not but they seem to be the exception rather than the rule. This being said, there are still some changes, that if implemented, would make a good poker room even better. Following are four suggestions that I believe will benefit not only the players, but the cardrooms as well.

Suggestion No. 1: Don't let players move two places for free. Many Nevada cardrooms allow players in hold'em and Omaha games to move past two live opponents without having to post a blind. The problem is that a few people abuse this privilege. As an example, suppose you are playing $10-$20 hold'em. This game has $15 in blinds and usually 10 players. Consequently every time you move two places, you gain approximately $3. Make a bunch of moves in a session, and your gain begins to add up. (Actually, you probably will gain much more than $3 because the later positions, which you are usually moving to, are theoretically worth more than the early positions.)

Most cardrooms in California don't allow free moves in games that require blinds. If you move, you must either wait the appropriate number of hands or post an appropriate blind. Needless to say, this stops the abuse and thus in my opinion, is a far superior system.

Suggestion No. 2: Don't consolidate games unless it is absolutely necessary. Sometimes games go short-handed, and if there is more than one game at the same stakes, the floor personnel often will try to consolidate them. In my opinion, games should be consolidated only if the players request it; otherwise they should be left alone.

The reason for this is that the consolidation interruption often causes people to quit playing. Now instead of two short-handed games, there may not be enough players left for even one game.

Worse, often the player (or players) who quits is a live one. Usually this happens when he is ahead and decides that he is satisfied with his win and doesn't want to be bothered with a table change, or he realizes that he is now too tired to get up and walk to the other table. I have seen many good games ruined because someone on the floor is "conscientious." Sometimes I wish that those of you who work the floor would be less helpful to those of us who are currently playing.

Suggestion No. 3: Allow players to play all hands that they pay for. Almost all cardrooms insist that if you are going to change tables, whether you are just transferring to another game of the same type and stakes or are going to a different game, that you do so immediately. This presents no problem in games where there is only an ante, but it *is* a problem in games where you must post a blind.

It seems to me that if you pay for hands, you should be allowed to play them. Yet most cardrooms insist that you move immediately. Even though I don't think this is right, I can see their point if you are playing in a game that has a time collection and if it is time to pay the collection. Now if you don't move immediately, the cardroom might lose a fee. But in rake games, this situation does not exist.

By the way, my suggestion also applies to play-overs, which often help keep a game going. If you are playing over and have just taken the blind, you should not be told by either the returning player or someone on the floor that you cannot play the full round.[6]

---

[6]I have actually changed my position on this. When you decide to change tables, you do so at your own request. Not moving immediately may cause the new incoming player a long wait, which is not fair to him. I now believe that if a player requests a transfer (or is playing over) he should be allowed to play his blinds and the button, but must then get up and make the change or forfeit the transfer.

Suggestion No. 4: Penalize players who play their small blinds late. Sometimes a player will take his big blind but then get up from the table on his little blind, only to return later to post his little blind from a late position. I am convinced that there is an advantage to this, namely, that it is now going to cost 25 percent less to try to steal the blinds. This is especially valuable in a tight game, particularly if the blinds do not play back very often. This can be stopped by making the late small blind dead. In other words, require the poster to put a full bet into the pot if he wants to play. I haven't seen much abuse of the little blind in the past couple of years, mainly because the room where I currently play does not allow it. Before that, however, several players engaged in this practice constantly, so I believe cardrooms should change their rules to guard against it.

Two Annoying
Player Practices

Two practices often go on at the poker tables that I believe need to be stopped or at least modified by appropriate rule changes. These practices are (1) frequently calling for new set-ups and (2) constantly insisting to see everyone's hand. Although these habitual requests are made by only a small number of players, they are nonetheless irritating. In addition, they hurt the games and reduce an expert player's earnings.

The main problem with frequently calling for new set-ups is that it slows down the game. This means that the expert player will now play fewer hands and make less money. This is even more pronounced in a time game, which is common in many California cardrooms, than in a rake game.

But there is another, even more important reason why the expert player will make less money: The long pause while the set-up is called for, then inspected, and finally thoroughly shuffled will allow some players who are currently steaming enough time to recover and play well again. As we all know, good players win most of their money from bad players, and a bad player may be someone who plays poorly all the time or someone who occasionally plays poorly but at other times plays reasonably well. Why give a player on tilt a chance to be at his best again, especially if he is ready — and willing — to give away most of his chips.

There is, of course a good reason to change decks every now and then. Some players will mark the cards by crimping them, pressing a thumb nail into them, or doing something else to them. These marks may not be deliberate, but it is still best to change decks on the order of once every two hours or sooner if a damaged card is found. (In a game like razz, which has a bad reputation, it might be best to change the decks more frequently, perhaps once every hour.) However, changing decks every few minutes as occurs in some cases is way too often.

As much as I dislike frequent requests for new set-ups, I don't view this practice to be as bad as constantly asking to see other peoples' hands. The lookers will usually tell you that they just want to "see how you play," but I suspect that in most instances they are trying to needle their opponents, especially if they have just caught a miracle card and/or if the pot is extremely large.

There is a very good reason why better players should want this practice to disappear: Their poorer playing opponents may be embarrassed into playing better. Many people come to cardrooms to gamble. They know that some of the plays they make are losing plays, but the chance to outdraw a professional is appealing to them, even if making these plays cost them "a little" money in the long run. (Actually these plays will cost them a lot of money in the long run, but few weak players realize this.) However, if poor players are constantly forced to show their hands and "to prove" how stupid they are, many of them — if they don't quit the game altogether will tighten up and begin to play much better. Now who needs that!

Fortunately, there is a simple solution to this problem: Allow only those players who either make or call the final bet to look at an opponent's hand. Implementing such a rule would eliminate much of the current irritation and expense. (By the way, in the larger stud games at the Mirage, this currently is the rule.)

Suggestions for Professional Players

What characteristics define a professional poker player? Is he one of the superstars sitting in the high-limit games? Or is he one of the broke or semibroke players who constantly hang around the cardrooms looking for a stake.

One definition I subscribe to is that a professional player is someone who derives enough income from playing poker that if he did not have this income, his lifestyle would be significantly altered. While I agree with this definition, to me, a professional player is much more. He is also someone who behaves in a manner that is good for the games. What follows are a few suggestions in this area.

Suggestion No. 1: Keep the game moving. One of the keys to profitable poker is playing lots of hands. Over the same period of time, a fast-paced game can easily produce twice as many hands as a slow-paced game. This translates into twice the profit. Of course, the skill of the dealer has a lot to do with this, but how players act at the table also has a bearing on the speed of the game. If you are beat, you should quickly throw your hand away. When it is your turn, be ready to act. When a hand is over, don't complain about the results. Don't ask for new set-ups unless something is wrong with the cards. And finally, when you win a pot, don't insist on seeing your opponent's hand. Usually this is done only to needle someone else, and it slows the game down a great deal.

Suggestion No. 2: Don't try to discover what your opponent called with. When I first began to play draw poker, I called a one-card draw who had bet after the draw. My opponent turned over three cards — all sixes. I spread my hand, which contained three aces. My opponent then turned over his other two cards, a pair of queens, which gave him a full house. Obviously this player was trying to find out how weak a hand I would call with. If he had seen one pair or a small two pair, or if I had just conceded to his three sixes, valuable information would have been gained, allowing him to bet marginal hands into me for profit.

The problem with this type of play is that it may embarrass your opponent. One thing professional players need to understand is that many people come to cardrooms to gamble. They know that a lot of their plays are bad, but they make them anyway. If you embarrass them with trick plays, they may quit gambling, causing the game to tighten up.

Suggestion No. 3: Don't harass or blame the dealers. While I agree that some dealers need to improve their skills, badgering them does not remedy the situation and refusing to play because your unlucky dealer is now in the box is just plain silly. The cards are random, and just because you have had bad results with a particular dealer doesn't mean that you can expect the same poor results in the future. Your expectation is to do no better and no worse than you would do with any other dealer.

However, there is a problem with sitting out. Many poor players do not want to play if the game is short-handed, so your immature behavior may drive them from the game. In addition, most people come to cardrooms hoping for an enjoyable experience. They do not want to play with children. Consequently, if you don't drive them from the game, they will often tighten up and quit gambling.

Suggestion No. 4: Don't lecture your opponents. One of the main reasons why professional players make money is that some of their opponents play very poorly. However, because there is a lot of luck in poker, especially in the short run, sometimes these bad players will draw out even when they are taking much the worse of it. Sure, these drawouts can be frustrating at times. But attempts to make them, which usually fail, are highly profitable for you, the pro. When this happens, either congratulate your opponent or don't say anything. A lecture explaining how stupid he is doesn't benefit you.

The pot is still lost, plus your opponent may now tighten up and quit gambling. And even worse, he might even learn something.

Final note: The best thing I know that can happen in a poker room is for a live one to walk in, see you playing in a game, and ask the floorman to put him in that game. There are some expert players who promote this situation all the time. Are you one of them?

A Few Thoughts On Tipping

Every now and then, the subject of tipping makes its way into the current poker literature. In fact, I have periodically read a number of essays on this topic in *The Card Player*. The authors have ranged from defending those players who almost never tip to giving ridiculous advice, such as in a $10-$20 game you should tip "a minimum of $1 for small pots and up to $5 for bigger pots," and "if you are running bad, toke the dealer before the deal starts."

One dealer told me that if players tipped this much, he would have to work only one day a week; and I suspect that if players *did* tip this much, dealers would be able to work only one day a week as there would not be many games since most players would quickly go broke. Which brings up another point. I believe that most people who try to play poker seriously do go broke, or at least are unable to make enough to support themselves and their families. This is true of many people I have known.

Even though the same familiar faces of successful pros are present in major cardrooms on most days, it needs to be pointed out that these people are the exception, not the rule. In reality, very few people are capable of mastering the game and then of having the discipline day in and day out to be a consistent winner. If you don't believe me, just look at all the dealers and floor personnel who were unable to make it as a poker pro.

The point is that if you are struggling at the poker table, advice to tip lavishly is probably not appreciated and certainly not considered. But even those players who are "stiffs" do contribute to dealers income. They form the core of most games, allowing them to be spread, which means that tourists will have a place to sit — and the best tips, of course, do come from tourists. Dealers who ridicule these nontippers and wish they would never show up have the wrong attitude.

Of course, there is a simple solution to this problem: *Tipping should not be allowed.* I believe that cardrooms (casinos) should pay their help a decent wage and should not expect their customers to do it for them. If this means that the rake (or collection) would have to be increased a small amount, then I am in favor of it. For example, in a $10-$20 hold'em game, I would have no objection to a maximum rake of $2.50 as opposed to the standard $2 if (1) the extra 50 cents was taken only when the pot got fairly large, meaning that it would amount to just a few extra dollars per hour, and (2) tipping was then prohibited. This idea also could apply to poker tournaments. Just charge a little extra juice and then do not allow the winners to tip.

Although I recognize that this is a radical idea, I believe that cardrooms adopting this policy, even as a temporary experiment, would be flooded with business. Additionally, I believe that players — even those who tip liberally — don't like the pressure of being expected to tip any more than dealers like being stiffed.

Finally, I don't expect my thoughts to solve the tipping controversy, and I'm sure that every so often it will pop up again. However, if some cardroom somewhere would increase its rake a small amount and outlaw tipping, we just might have the start of something new.

The Future of Poker

Despite ongoing problems in the cardroom industry, public poker is here to stay. But what games will be popular in the future? Will any of the games we currently play go the route of five-card stud and die out? Which games should we strive to become experts in so we can make lots of money in the future? And finally, which games should we not waste our time trying to master?

These are all interesting and important questions to those of us who play poker seriously. What follows are my opinions on the various poker games currently being spread in the major cardrooms of Nevada and California. Keep in mind that these are my opinions and someone else may see things quite differently.

Game No. 1: No-limit hold'em. The problem with no-limit hold'em is that the expert player has too great an edge over weak players and will virtually never lose to these people. Since bad players almost never win, they either go broke, find another game, or quit playing poker altogether. Unfortunately, there is not much future in no-limit hold'em.

Game No. 2: Pot-limit hold'em. My thoughts here are almost identical to the comments just given. In other words there is not much future in pot-limit hold'em.

Game No. 3: Limit hold'em. At the middle limits, more limit hold'em is played than any other game in the cardrooms of Nevada and California. I think the short-term luck factor in this game needs to be a little larger to make it ideal, but this game does contain an "illusion of action" like no other form of poker.[7] Consequently, limit hold'em may have the best future of all forms of poker.

---

[7] In some hold'em games where a great deal of money is going into the pot early, this statement is no longer true.

Game No. 4: Seven-card stud. Stud always has maintained a reasonable amount of popularity, and it should. The game is a marvelous blend of luck and skill, although I believe the luck factor is a little too large to make it ideal. This is especially true at the big limits, where the ante is proportionately larger and even the expert will go through large fluctuations. Stud hasn't caught on as quickly as hold'em in California, perhaps because the game looks extremely complicated, but its popularity is starting to rise. Consequently, seven-card stud should have a good future, though not quite as good as hold'em.

Game No. 5: Limit Omaha. If ever there was a worthless game, this is it. The luck factor is too great, and the skill factor is too minimal. In Las Vegas, I know of only a few cardrooms that regularly spread limit Omaha, and these games seem to be getting slowly weaker. I don't believe this game has a future.

Game No. 6: Pot limit Omaha. This form of poker is more interesting and requires more skill than the limit version, but it suffers from the same problems that no-limit and pot-limit hold'em suffer from. That is, the suckers quickly get killed, and there seem to be fewer suckers every day. Pot-limit Omaha will still live at the major tournaments and occasionally will be spread in the big cardrooms, but the games should slowly get worse. I believe there is still some money to be made in the game, but this may not be true a few years from now.

Game No. 7: Omaha, eight or better. This is the surprise game on the list, and I believe it is slowly growing in popularity. Part of the reason for this is that if you play the game extremely badly, your luck factor will be quite large. Consequently, terrible players can go for a long time before they begin to realize that they don't play this game very well. This is because they win money from other terrible players, not from the experts. I believe Omaha, eight or better may have a good future, even though it will never approach hold'em or stud in popularity.

Game No. 8: Razz. This is seven-card stud played for low. The game is simple and has about the right amount of short-term luck. However, razz has a bad reputation for cheating and is spread only in a small number of places. I believe there will always be a razz game somewhere, but it never will be a major force in poker and never will have the popularity it once enjoyed.

Game No. 9: High draw. The version I am referring to is jacks or better to open, played with a joker. Unfortunately, this game is too slow and does not have a high enough element of short-term luck. Most games quickly disappeared in California once hold'em and stud became available. There is still a little high draw played in California, but I suspect it won't be too long before it is almost all gone.

Game No. 10: Ace-to-five lowball. This is the standard draw game played for low. Unlike high draw, it has survived the hold'em and stud invasion, but is slowly losing its popularity. I believe the reason for this is that four or five betting rounds are just more interesting than two. There are still a lot of games around, but with most new players going to hold'em or stud, the lowball games are becoming very tough to beat.

Game No. 11: Seven-card stud, eight or better. At the time of this writing, this is the game I know the least about. I suspect there will always be some eight or better played, but I don't have a good feel for how well the game will do when compared to other forms of poker and whether there will be a lot of money to be made in it in the future.

Omaha Is Dead!

What's wrong with limit Omaha hold'em? During the past few years I have seen many predictions stating that this form of poker will become the game of the future. Yet, as far as I know, there are only a few small-limit games spread in all of Las Vegas on a regular basis. In addition, very few games are being spread in the cardrooms of California, even though many places have tried to promote this form of poker. How can this be? Isn't Omaha supposed to be the most exciting form of poker ever developed? Isn't it true that once you play this form of poker, you never return to conventional hold'em or stud or lowball or whatever game you regularly play?

The answer is no. Omaha is not the terrific game it has been cracked up to be. And I think I know why this game seems to turn players off.

However, before explaining what is wrong with Omaha, I want to point out that some fairly good games appear at the major tournaments. This is often because some players sit down who essentially have no idea of how the game should be played. The major tournaments also get pretty good turnouts for their Omaha events. But I think some of these tournaments could offer anything and have pretty good turnouts. On the other hand, I see few small Omaha tournaments run on a weekly basis.

So why is Omaha virtually dead? And why is this future form of poker not looking forward to a very good future? I believe the reason is that it's too easy to make the nuts in this game. Once anyone has some experience at Omaha, he quickly learns to draw for the nuts or (in many cases) to throw his hand away. This means that you cannot punish your opponents for making mistakes, since experienced Omaha players just make very few mistakes. (Compare this game to conventional hold'em, where some players — who have years of experience still make numerous basic mistakes.)

This means that everyone quickly plays about equally; that is, even the best players will have low win rates. But what about the standard deviation? (Remember, the standard deviation is the statistical measurement of luck that I so often refer to.) Because of the large drawout potential in this game, it is probably quite high. Consequently, the skilled Omaha player can't have a (true) high win rate, but will go through many large swings. Who wants to play in a game like this?

Digressing for a moment, I do not know of any cardrooms that spread wild-card games. You can't play deuces wild in Las Vegas, unless you play it at home. But it seems to me that Omaha is the closest thing to having a wild-card game spread in a public cardroom. Players are just not interested in games where the element of skill is kept to a minimum. They want games where there is a good balance between skill and luck, and limit Omaha does not meet this criterion.

So what's the bottom line? It's this: *If you are interested in playing poker, learn how to play a game that has good prospects. This includes games like Texas hold'em, seven-card stud, and even ace-to-five lowball.* Omaha will not dominate the poker scene in the future. In my opinion, it will remain as sort of a novelty game that will get some low-limit play, but at best, will be spread only sporadically in most cardrooms. So the next time you read an article about how terrific this form of limit poker is, just ignore it. It won't be accurate. Remember, the real money will be made by those people who become experts at the games that offer good prospects.

And what if you are running a cardroom? Again limit Omaha is probably not worthwhile spreading. It will not maintain the interest of your players, plus the hands take so long to play, your drop will be reduced when compared to the standard games.

In the Old Days

How should trouble makers be handled in a card room? I'm sure numerous ways have been tried, but a good solution to this problem is not always easy to come by. But the following story describes a method that was used many years ago. And while I don't recommend it to today's cardroom managers, it did seem quite effective.

A gambler in camp named Ike Morris had a local reputation as a mean man with a gun. One day while (Wyatt) Earp was absent, Morris sat down at his (faro) table, placed a pile of bills on a card, and told Wyatt's dealer to turn. After a few turns, the card won for the bank and the dealer picked up the wagered money. Morris immediately set up a howl, claiming the cards were crooked, and demanded his money back. The dealer replied that he was not authorized to return the bet, that he only worked for wages, and that Morris must see Wyatt Earp if he had a complaint. When Earp returned, Morris confronted him, insisting that he had been cheated and demanding restitution. Wyatt heard him out and said that he would talk to his employee about the problem. He conferred with the dealer and was assured that the cards were honest and Morris had been given a square deal. By now the word had spread that a showdown was imminent between the two gunmen, with fireworks likely, and a large crowd had gathered.

Wyatt walked back to where Morris waited. "You were right," he said. The dealer had admitted cheating, continued Earp, and for that reason he felt very much like returning Morris's money. "However," he went on, "you are looked upon in these parts as something of a bad man, and if I give you back your money it will be said that you made me do it. Therefore, I am going to keep it."

The next move was up to Morris. He stared at Earp for a few moments, then laughed nervously and offered to buy drinks. His reputation destroyed, and unable to cope with this obloquy, Morris vanished from Gunnison a few days later.

What's the best poker hand? If you are playing high, most people will tell you that it's a royal flush, assuming there are no wild cards. If you are playing low, the reply you probably will get is that the best hand is a wheel or a bicycle. However, as the following story illustrates, the best poker hand actually may be quite different from what most people think. Notice that this hand will always win, no matter what the game.

On another occasion, when (Wild Bill) Hickok was in danger of being cleaned out by a pair of crooked poker sharks, he called the largest raise of the evening with his last greenbacks. At the showdown one of his opponents displayed the winning hand and Bill tossed in his cards. "Hold it!" he said, as the sharper reached for the pot. Drawing two revolvers, he leveled them at the swindlers. "I have a pair of sixes and they beat anything." The slicks watched glumly as Hickok cleared the table.

Both of these anecdotes come from *Knights of the Green Cloth, The Saga of Frontier Gamblers* by Robert K. DeArment. The book is a detailed history of the gamblers of the Old West, "the good guys, the bad guys, and their women — wives, mistresses, and colleagues in gambling establishments." Although reading this book won't improve your poker strategy, it will provide many hours of entertainment.

In The Cardrooms

Afterthought

As can be seen, this area of poker, which is usually neglected in most of the poker literature, is extremely important. Having good games available is absolutely essential to serious poker players. Without good games, don't expect to be successful, no matter how well you happen to play.

Most serious players need to remember that the way they behave will influence those decisions cardrooms make that affect how well players can expect to do. An attitude like "getting even with the dealers one blue bird at a time" just hurts everyone, and those players who exhibit this type of characteristic are hurting themselves most of all in the long run.

On the other hand, cardrooms also need to do their part. Although they shouldn't allow their regular players to behave poorly, they do need to run an organized and efficient room that promotes poker. Most rooms in operation today do just that. As the essays have implied, those rooms that fail in this area don't stay in business.

Part Eight
Poker Quizzes

Poker Quizzes

Introduction

Now we come to four poker quizzes that concern four hands I actually played. I think these hands not only are more interesting than the typical poker hand but also require appropriate reasoning and logic to play optimally. Take the quizzes and try to figure out the correct play. If you come up with the same answers I did, you might consider yourself an expert — at least for these four problems.

Quiz No. 1

You are playing in a $10-$20 hold'em game. The game is 10-handed, and the blinds are $5 and $10. Several people have just called the blind, and you are on the button with a very marginal

You also call and the flop comes

Everyone checks to you, and you bet. Now everyone folds except a loose, wild, and reckless player who is on your immediate right and who (to your surprise) check-raises. You call. The next card is the

Your opponent bets into you, you raise, and he calls. The final card is the

Again to your surprise, your opponent bets into you. What is the correct play for you to make? (Stop and try to come up with the answer before continuing.)

To figure out what the correct play is, you must first determine what hand your opponent probably has. Only calling before the flop after several people are already in shows that his initial starting hand was not very strong. However, since he was able to check-raise on the flop, it is likely that he did make something. But is that something a straight draw? Probably not since (1) he most likely would have bet the flop in the hope that either everyone would fold or he would get several callers, and (2) his check may have indicated that he was not that worried about a free card. Consequently, he probably has made either a pair of aces, two pair, or a set.

The next clue comes when your opponent only calls your raise on the turn. If he had made a set or two pair on the flop, which has now become a full house, he most likely would have played back at you (or perhaps tried for a check-raise on the river). Hence it is clear that you are probably looking at a pair of aces, which has now become two pair with the sevens on board. (Your opponent also may have flopped aces and sixes. However, if this is the case, the board pairing sevens has "counterfeited" his pair of sixes.) Also, your opponent probably has called your raise hoping either that you are bluffing, perhaps with a draw, or that you also have an ace (which means that if he can't win outright, he might be able to split the pot with you.)

However, when your opponent bets into you on the river, it Indicates that the nine must have improved his hand. Since it also appears likely that he started with an ace in his hand, it now seems almost certain that your opponent started with an ace-nine. His hand is probably not suited, because with a suited ace-nine he would have been more inclined to raise before the flop. Consequently, the correct play is to raise again.

By the way, it is unlikely that your opponent made nines full on the river. For him to have this hand, it would mean that he check-raised you with an underpair on the flop. This is also extremely doubtful since (1) his call before the flop does not indicate a hand as strong as a pair of nines, (2) he would be hesitant to try for a check raise with an ace on board, and (3) supposing he had a pair of nines, it would be improbable for him to check on the flop in his late position and give a free card that could easily beat him, assuming that he does have the best hand.

Quiz No. 2

You are playing in a $10-$20 hold'em game. The game is 10-handed, and the blinds are $5 and $10. A wild, reckless player has called up front, everyone passes to you in a late position, and you hold

You raise, and the big blind calls, as well as the original caller. The flop comes

Everyone checks to you. Since it is unlikely that anyone would have a piece of this flop, you bet (hoping to pick up the pot), but both of your opponents call. The next card is the

Again both of your opponents check to you, and you bet hoping that you were just called by overcards who will now fold. (Notice that

this bet is somewhat risky. If one of your opponents has an ace, it is unlikely that he will throw his hand away since he will now think that his chances of having the best hand have gone up.) However, as before, no one folds. The final card is the

which now gives you top pair. The person in the blind position checks, but the wild, reckless player who is next to act bets. What is the correct play for you to make? (Stop and think before going on with the quiz.)

To figure out what the correct play is, you must first determine what hand your opponents have (or don't have). First, let's consider the player who just bet. Since he only called on the flop and on the turn, it is doubtful that he has a three or a five. He most likely would have tried for a check-raise on one of the earlier rounds (usually fourth street with most players) if he held one of these cards. (This is also true of your other opponent.) However, his bet does indicate strength, which seems to signify that the queen hit him.

This means that we need to figure out his kicker. Because of his aggressive nature, it is unlikely that he would have just called before the flop if his kicker was either an ace or a king. Consequently, he has either the same hand you have or a weaker hand, such as queen-ten or queen-nine or perhaps even something like queen-rag suited.

As for the player in the big blind, you don't need to worry very much about him. First, if he had a queen, as does your other opponent, he might have bet. Second, you have now accounted for three queens, making it doubtful that this player also holds a queen. Consequently, he can be ignored, and your correct play is to raise.

Let's make two other points. Suppose you had a different hand, such as two jacks. Even though it is likely that you are now up against a queen, this doesn't mean that you should fold. Notice that the pot has become fairly large. If there is a moderate chance that the bettor is bluffing — and this is likely with a wild, reckless opponent — then a call is correct.

If a blank hits on the end, you did not improve, and it was checked to you, bluffing is probably incorrect for two reasons. First, if either of your opponents holds an ace — and this is moderately probable since one of them called a raise cold before the flop — he will call, hoping to split the pot. Second, even if there is no ace out, there is a reasonable chance that you are beat anyway. For both of your opponents to call twice with such a low board, the possibility certainly exists that someone has better than two overcards .

If a king hits on the end, and it is checked to you, then bluffing does becomes a viable option. This is because you have played your hand in a fashion that indicates you may be holding a king. It is now much more difficult for someone to call you down with only an ace or a small pair.

Another concept is present here that I have never seen discussed in print before, and that often comes into play in hold'em-type games: It is important to raise on the end if there is a good chance that your opponent who has bet has the same hand you have but is unlikely to have a better hand. The reason for raising is that this may make your opponent fold, and instead of splitting the pot, you get to keep it all. Notice that in the situation just described, this is the case. There a good probability that your opponent might now fold queen-jack. And if he does, raising is a very profitable play indeed.

Quiz No. 3

You are playing in an eight-handed, $15-$30 seven-card stud game with a $2 ante and a $5 bring-in. A player in early position with a king up calls the five dollars, a middle-position player with an ace up raises, the upcards thrown away are the 5♠, 2♣, 2♦, 6♥, and the Q♠, and you are in a late position with

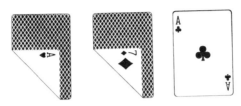

You reraise, and both players call. Both of your opponents are experienced, conservative players, though neither is considered an expert. Notice that it looks like the player in early position with the king up probably has a three-flush, although he might have a pair of kings.

On fourth street, everyone catches a blank, you bet, and both of your opponents call. The exact same thing happens on fifth street, meaning that it is now likely the player with the king up started with two kings since it does not appear possible that he could have a draw. (If he has not improved his three-flush, he would certainly throw his hand away for a big bet.)

On sixth street, you and the other player who started with an ace up both catch blanks, but the player with a king showing makes a small pair (meaning that he probably has kings up). The boards now look as follows:

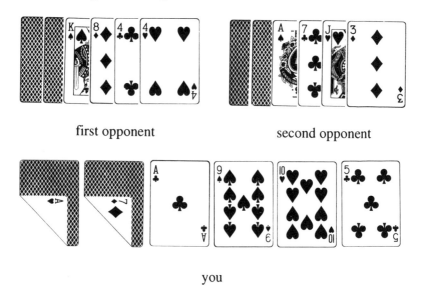

first opponent   second opponent

you

Other dead cards: 5♠ 2♣ 2♦ 6♥ Q♠

The player with the small pair showing checks, even though he is
likely to have kings up; the second player checks; and now it is your
turn. Notice that the player with kings up is probably afraid to bet
since he does not want to be raised if someone has made aces up (or
better). What should you do? (Stop and think before going on.)

Your play is to bet. Should you improve your hand, it most likely
will be good. There are 11 cards that will improve your hand (one
ace, two sevens, three tens, three nines, and two fives.) and 22 cards
that will not help you. Notice that your chance of improvement is 2-
to-1 against you and that your chance of finishing with the best hand
is a little more than 2-to-1. This means that your bet is essentially
free in terms of expectation; that is, in the long run, these kinds of
bets will cost you very little. Consequently, it does not seem to
matter whether you make this bet or not.

But it does matter, as this bet may put you into position to steal
the pot on the river. Some players are willing to call once if they
think you might be bluffing, but they will not call twice since it

becomes doubtful in their minds that you would have the nerve to twice bet with an inferior hand.

This means that you should not only bet on sixth street but also be prepared to bet on the river whether you improve or not. When you do improve, you probably will have the best hand and will win the majority of the time you are called, so you certainly should bet. When you don't improve, you should still bet even if there is only a small chance of stealing the pot. This is because the pot has become so large that even if your bluff is only occasionally successful, it is still well worth trying. The only time you should check on the river is when you are absolutely certain you will be called. Otherwise, the bluff becomes correct. Notice that we are looking at a situation where it is correct both to bluff and to bet for value.

Quiz No. 4

You are playing in an eight-handed, $15-$30 seven-card stud game with a $2 ante and a $5 bring-in. A player in early position with the 8♦ up calls the $5 bring-in, and you are in a middle position with

Before you can act, another player with the J♠ up throws his hand away. The player on your immediate left has a king up, which is the only upcard higher than your jack. What is your play?

Clearly, it is to raise. However, if the player showing the king reraises, you almost always should fold unless this is a player who would be likely to bluff in this spot. (Even then, calling may be only marginally correct at best. The reason for this is explained later.)

You raise, the player showing the king folds, but your next opponent, who shows the 6♣, reraises. Now the bring-in, who has the 2♠ up, calls the double raise, and the original caller with the 8♦ also calls the double raise. Let's suppose that the player who reraised is the type of player who would be just as likely to reraise with a hand like

as he would with a hand like

254

(In this case, reraising with a pair of sixes is not really so bad. Since your opponent's kicker is high and his hand is live, he definitely wants to play, and it might be best to play heads-up.) What is your play?

First, notice that there is a good chance you have the best hand on third street. But also notice that your hand is not very live. Not only is a deuce that matches your kicker already out, but a jack is dead as well. In addition, your kicker is small. This means that it will be difficult for you to make a hand better than jacks up. Moreover, in a multiway pot that already has a lot of money in it (which implies that your opponents are probably prepared to go a long way with their hands), it is doubtful that a hand as weak as jacks up (which you may not be able to make) can take down the money.

Consequently, the correct play is to throw your hand away, even though the pot is currently offering you odds of approximately 8-to-1. Remember, seven-card stud, as its name implies, is a seven-card game. Even if you were 100 percent sure that you had the best hand on third street, it still would be correct to throw your hand away. This is true despite the large pot odds you are getting. I suspect, however, that few players are capable of doing this.

Playing hands that are not live is probably the major error made by most regular stud players. There is no question that it is difficult to throw a hand away on third street that at first glance looks reasonably good. Yet consistently doing so in these spots is one of the skills that separates the experts from the rest of the crowd. It is important to recognize that even though your current pot odds may appear quite positive, your overall implied odds, which are the odds that really count, are very negative.

Poker Quizzes

Afterthought

In this section, I have given quizzes on two hold'em hands and two stud hands, and I have presented the reasoning behind how I think they should have been played. Am I right? Did I give the correct answers to my quizzes? And would you have played the hands the same way I did?

Arriving at answers different from those I gave doesn't mean that you are not an expert player. As I have stated many times before, and as most of us know, poker is a complicated game. Although it is possible that my answers are wrong, I suspect that they are correct in many situations. But against a different player, who is sitting in a different line-up, whose perception of me is different from what I think it is, and so forth, my answers might be totally wrong.

When thinking about poker, always try to maintain flexibility in your decisions. No strategy, no matter how correct or precise it may seem, is set in concrete. This is especially true in games as complicated as hold'em and stud. Constantly making adjustments to your play in general is one of the keys to being an expert player, and staying one step ahead of your competition is absolutely essential to winning play.

One thing to keep in mind when reviewing these quizzes, or when sitting at the poker table and a tricky situation comes up, is to select the strategy that should produce the most profit in the long run. This is not necessarily the strategy that might win the most pots for you. In fact, it might be a strategy that never wins a pot for you; in other words, the correct play may be to throw your hand away, meaning that in the long run you lose less in this spot. Very few players I know think in these terms, but those who do are quite successful.

Needless to say, when a tough situation does comes up, you never have a lot of time to think about it. However, spending time reviewing tough hands when you are away from the poker table can help you make the right decisions when you are in action.

Another thing to remember is that there is more to poker than just looking at your hand. Many players make a decision about the cards that they are holding and never take into account other information that may be available. This can lead to some disasters. For example, a full house in hold'em is usually a strong hand, but if your full house is the small end of two pair on board, your hand may not be worth much. Many players flop a three-of-a-kind when a small pair appears, only to see the high card pair on the river. They then lose a whole bunch of bets when their hand is just worth a "crying call." Has this ever happened to you? If this is the type of trap you find yourself falling into, then your game needs a lot of work.

Notice that when taking the quizzes, it was important to understand what the other available information meant. For example, in the second seven-card stud quiz, if your hand had been live instead of dead, the correct decision would have been to call instead of to throw the hand away.

Yet most players don't take this available information into account because they are either unaware of it, don't realize its importance, or are just not willing to do the mental work it requires.

Again, as I have stated many times before, poker is not an easy game. If it were, there would be no experts because everyone would play approximately the same. It would take just three to six weeks to master a game, and only the house would make any money. In fact, I doubt that even cardrooms would make money since there would not be as many games as there are today. But fortunately, this is not the case.

Conclusion

Perhaps the most important idea this text has stressed is that to be a good poker player — or a good gambler, for that matter — you must do your homework. Poker is a complex game. If you don't do the right amount of thinking and studying, plus a fair amount of playing, don't expect to be very successful.

I constantly meet people who introduce themselves to me and tell me that they have read books I have either written or co-authored and how much good these materials have done them. But what is interesting is that when I watch these people play, most of them at best play very poorly. The moral: One quick reading of a good poker book might pump you up, but it won't make you into a world-class player.

It is only occasionally that I see a new player who plays well and who probably has a good future in front of him. But promising players do come along, and I think there should be more of them. I believe the reason there are so few is that most people will not invest the time — and this time can sometimes be boring — that is required to master these games at an expert level.

Another reason I believe so many people fail is that they have too much gamble in them. If you are always trying to find a creative way to play your hands, especially if you always want to play your hands fast, you will have trouble winning more than a marginal amount. This doesn't mean that creative plays are not a necessary part of winning poker. In fact, I don't believe you can be a winner in most games, especially once you leave the small limits, without them. However, there are too many self-proclaimed world-class players, who often state that they are "the best player in Las Vegas," but, who in fact just struggle.

Although they may have an occasional big night, because of the larger standard deviation these people play with, you would expect them to have more of these big nights than a lot of consistent winners. But they also have more horrendous losses, which means that in the long run they usually are not very successful.

I hope this book, along with the others I have either written or co-authored, will be of help to you. But remember, poker is not easy. However, if you are willing to do the necessary work — and some of you are — it can be a very rewarding profession.

Appendix A

Recommended Poker Books

There are a few poker books that I consider absolutely must reading for anyone striving for success in this game. The following is a list of these books, along with some comments about each of them. Anyone interested in my opinion on other gambling books, including those on poker, should consult *Gambling Theory and Other Topics.*

1. *Super System — A Course in Power Poker* **by Doyle Brunson.** This text is considered a classic source of information on most major limit games played as well as on no-limit hold'em. The book was written by two-time World Champion Doyle Brunson in collaboration with some of the best players in the world, including Mike Caro, David Sklansky, Chip Reese, and Bobby Baldwin. Most serious poker players, myself included, will literally wear the cover off their copies. My only criticism of the book is that as years go by, it has become somewhat outdated. For instance, most high-low split games are played today with a qualifier for low, and the excellent high-low split section in Brunson's book does not discuss this concept.

2. *The Theory of Poker* **by David Sklansky.** This is one of the best books ever written on poker, and it was written by a top professional player. Unlike Brunson's *Super System,* it is not a "how-to" book but a book on theory that discusses in depth strategy and many sophisticated concepts. Serious players who do not study this book will lag behind those players who do. I reread my copy every three or four months and always find it helpful to my game.

3. *Hold'em Poker* by David Sklansky. The first definitive work on the game of hold'em poker, this book is absolutely must reading for anyone planning to play in either California or Nevada. The book covers not only the basics, such as what hands to start with, but also very sophisticated play. The only criticism I have of this book is that it is somewhat outdated in the sense that most games today are structured a little differently from what this text is geared for. Even so, anyone who reads and studies this book will be way ahead of those who don't.

4. *Hold'em Poker For Advanced Players* by David Sklansky and Mason Malmuth. For today's modern game, this book offers the strongest strategy ever put into print. Anyone who studies this text, is well-disciplined, and gets the proper experience should become a significant winner. Some of the ideas covered include play on the first two cards, semi-bluffing, the free card, inducing bluffs, being beat on the river, staying with a draw, playing when a pair flops, playing trash hands, fourth-street play, playing in loose games, playing in short-handed games, and much more.

5. *Seven Card Stud For Advanced Players* by David Sklansky, Mason Malmuth, and Ray Zee. The comments given for *Hold'em Poker For Advanced Players* also apply to this text. Some of the ideas covered include: the cards that are out, ante stealing, playing big pairs, reraising the possible bigger pair, playing small and medium pairs, playing the three-flush, playing the three-straight, playing weak hands, fourth street, pairing your door card on fourth street, fifth street, sixth street, seventh street, defending against the possible ante steal, playing against a paired door card, continuing with a draw, scare-card strategy, buying the free card on fourth street, playing in tightly structured games, playing in loose games, playing in short-handed games, and much more.

6. *High-Low-Split Poker, Seven-Card Stud and Omaha Eight-or-Better For Advanced Players* by Ray Zee. This is actually the third book in the "For Advanced Players" series but in reality it is really two books in one. Some of the ideas discussed in the seven-card stud eight-or-better section include starting hands, disguising your hand on third street, when an ace raises, fourth street, fifth street, sixth street, seventh street, position, bluffing, staying to the end, scare cards, and much more. Some of the ideas discussed in the Omaha eight-or-better section include general concepts, position, low hands, high hands, your starting hand, how to play your hand, play on the flop, multiway versus short handed play, scare cards, getting counterfeited, your playing style, and much more

7. *Caro's Book of Tells* by Mike Caro. This text is the definitive work on tell play — that is on how to interpret the body language of poker — and should be read by all serious poker players. The book contains more than 250 photographs, as well as detailed descriptions of what is happening and the motivation behind each tell.

8. *Gambling Theory and Other Topics* by Mason Malmuth. This text is absolutely must reading for all serious players. The theme of the book is the dynamic concept of non-self-weighting gambling strategies. Also included is the most accurate advice ever published on fluctuations, bankroll requirements, and poker tournament strategies.

Appendix B

Supplemental Reading

Although the following books are not as important as those listed in Appendix A, most serious poker players will want to study them. Notice that some of these texts do not focus on poker.

1. *Sklansky on Poker* by David Sklansky. This text is a combination of *Sklansky on Razz* and *Essays on Poker*, with much new material added. Specifically, this book contains the definitive work on the game of razz (seven-card stud played for low), many essays on general poker concepts, and a short section on tournament play. Anyone who reads and studies this book not only will improve his overall play, but also should be able to play razz virtually perfectly.

2. *Caro's Fundamental Secrets of Poker...and Seminar Playbook* by Mike Caro. I don't agree with everything this text contains, but many of Caro's best concepts are discussed. At the very least, this book will give you a lot to think about, and at best, it definitely will improve your game. Topics covered include general winning advice, seven-card stud, Texas hold'em, tells and psychology, and tournament advice.

3. *Poker For Women* by Mike Caro. This book is an interesting work for beginning players with a special emphasis on the advantages female players have in a mostly male game. Even though it is written for someone just starting out in poker, this text should be read by most serious players.

4. *Poker Essays, Vol. II* by Mason Malmuth. If you like the book that you have just read, then you should also like this text. It is a compilation of the articles that I wrote from 1991 to 1996. Topics include moving up, why the best players sometimes go broke, poker skills, playing 15 percent, adjusting to the big ante, cardroom theory, and erroneous concepts.

5. *Winning Concepts in Draw and Lowball* by Mason Malmuth. This book is written for both the amateur and the professional player. It is partitioned into sections designed to help players improve their skills and it teaches one how to think like a top player, which is absolutely essential to winning play. Topics include poker reasons, basic mistakes, basic strategy, advanced strategy, killing the pot, psychology, and advanced plays.

6. *The Biggest Game in Town* by A. Alvarez. This entertaining text is about the World Series of Poker and some of the more famous players who regularly participate in that event. The book won't help you play any better, but I found it to be very enjoyable reading.

7. *Play Poker, Quit Work, And Sleep Till Noon* by John Fox. This book is controversial and somewhat out-of-date because of the changed conditions in most California cardrooms. And although it is only about high draw, I still consider this text must reading for all serious players, no matter what their game, as it discusses aspects of poker strategy not covered in many other places.

8. *Omaha Hold'em Poker (The Action Game)* by Bob Ciaffone. This is an excellent book, written by a professional player, that offers accurate advice for the relatively new games of Omaha and Omaha high-low split, eight or better. Anyone who studies this text, is well-disciplined, and does not play too big should have no trouble winning.

9. *Poker Faces. The Life and Work of Professional Card Players* by David Hayano. Written by a top player, this book is a fascinating account of the lives and experiences of professional card players. The book won't help you play better since it does not address strategy, but it should be read by anyone interested in taking up the game of poker seriously.

10. *Poker Strategy, Winning With Game Theory* **by Nesmith Ankeny.** This is an excellent book on draw poker and is based on a game-theory approach. Many strategic concepts are also discussed, and I consider this book must reading for most serious players.

11. *Total Poker* **by David Spanier.** This is another book that won't necessarily help your game but will provide lots of entertainment.

12. *Winning Poker Systems* **by Norman Zadeh.** This book is absolutely must reading for all serious players. Although I think some of the opening tables are too loose, this work discusses many strategic concepts that are not covered well in other places. It is an excellent source of poker theory as well.

13. *The Education of a Poker Player* **by Herbert O. Yardley.** This is an ancient book that contains much outdated advice. However, I believe Yardley was a good poker player, and some excellent insights are present in this book. Make sure you read it, but learn the specifics on strategy from another source.

14. *Seven-Card Stud, The Waiting Game* **by George Percy.** The information this text contains won't be enough to win at medium and high stakes, but the book is well-written and is very good for beginners at seven-card stud.

15. *Omaha Express* **by Michael J. Barry.** I was quite surprised by the quality of this book since I did not like the hold'em book written by the same author. The text is only a small part of the book, which contains mostly tables. I don't see the value in most of the tables, but the advice on how to play is pretty good. For example, the author warns about queen-high flush draws, bottom sets, bottom two pair, and the danger of having some of your outs in your hand.

16. *Getting the Best of It* **by David Sklansky.** This is another marvelous book by David Sklansky that is absolutely must reading no matter what area of gambling you are interested in. The book contains an excellent section on sports betting, as well as essays on both poker and blackjack. Also included in the text is one of the best descriptions of the mathematics of gambling for those of you who are not mathematicians.

17. *Caro on Gambling* **by Mike Caro.** This very good and readable book covers gambling in general and contains many profound statements. It includes four crash courses for different poker games, video poker advice, and advice (similar to my own) on money management. All in all, this book contains some of Caro's best material.

18. *The Mathematics of Gambling* **by Edward O. Thorp.** A well-written book discussing many interesting gambling topics, this text is certainly worth reading. The advice on "bet sizing" is extremely valuable.

19. *Theory of Gambling and Statistical Logic* **by Richard Epstein.** I consider this to be one of the most amazing books in the gambling field. It is a graduate-level text for those with a sophisticated background in math and statistics, and is filled with a wealth of information.

20. *Gambling and the Law* **by I. Nelson Rose.** A well-written and interesting book about gambling law by the leading authority in the field. This book should be read by all serious gamblers.

21. *Gambling Scams* **by Darwin Ortiz.** A well-written text by a most knowledgeable expert. This book covers many different forms of cheating in all sorts of gambling games and environments. This work is absolutely must reading for all serious gamblers.

22. ***The Mathematics of Games and Gambling* by Edward Packel.** This book provides an excellent discussion of the mathematics and probability that is important to gambling. The book is enjoyable to read and is filled with many helpful examples. I highly recommend it for those of you who are weak in this area.

23. ***Inside the Poker Mind: Essays on Hold 'em and General Poker Concepts* by John Feeney, Ph.D.** Poker is a game of many skills and to become an expert poker player you need to master them all. This includes concepts such as hand selection, position, proper image projection, and reading hands. However, there are many players who have mastered most of these skills yet they still do poorly in the games — at best they are only small winners. And when they step up in limit and challenge the better players, they almost always fail. This text shows that winning poker is a process that requires a lot of thinking as well as a thorough and systematic approach to the game. If you are serious about your game, and hope to have success at the middle and high limits, this book is a must read.

24. ***The Psychology of Poker* by Alan N. Schoonmaker, Ph. D.** To be successful at poker you cannot win just by "doing what comes naturally." For example, have you ever wondered why some players seem extremely aggressive while others are passive? Why some are tight and others loose? Furthermore, have you ever wondered why some tactics seem to come naturally to you while others don't? This text will answer many of these questions. It will explain why you and your opponents play the way you do. The author also suggests strategic adjustments that you should make to improve your results against different types of players, and he suggests personal adjustments that will help you to play better and enjoy the game more. This text is especially helpful for those of you who are relatively new to poker.

25. *Poker Tournament Strategies* **by Sylvester Suzuki.** Poker tournaments are very different from conventional poker games, and there are few players who excel at both. But it can be done. This text is an excellent guide to those of you who want to get started with tournament play. It is especially helpful in the area of when it is correct to rebuy.

26. *Real Poker: The Cooke Collection* **by Roy Cooke.** This text is especially helpful to those of you who are interested in the thought processes of an expert player when he is at the table. Cooke is at his best when he is stepping through a hand.

Index

NOTES

NOTES